"WHEN WE DON'T HAVE THE WORDS
CHOCOLATE CAN SPEAK VOLUMES."

JOAN BAUER

I ♥ CHOCOLATE

MOUTHWATERING AND DELICIOUS CHOCOLATE RECIPES FROM MASTERS OF THE ART OF CHOCOLATE

BEVERLEY DUNKLEY ♥ DIRK SCHONKEREN ♥ IAIN BURNETT ♥ JOHN HUBER

JOHN SLATTERY ♥ MARK TILLING ♥ RUTH HINKS ♥ THIERRY DUMOUCHEL

I ♥ CHOCOLATE

First published in 2013 by Chef Books

Chef Books
Network House, 28 Ballmoor, Celtic Court,
Buckingham MK18 1RQ, UK
WWW.CHEFMAGAZINE.CO.UK

© Chef Books

ISBN: 978-1-908202-06-2

Printed by M.P. Printing in China

Publisher: Peter Marshall
Author: Shirley Marshall
Editors: Helen Homes
Photography: Ben Pollard, Myburgh du Plessis, Peter Marshall
Designer: Philip Donnelly

INTRODUCTION

WELCOME TO THE SUMPTUOUS WORLD OF CHOCOLATE.

With its enticing aroma, its brilliant sheen, its sensuous melt, there is nothing like it. Chocolate guarantees a moment of enchantment. There is a world of seduction in a delicate mousse, a melting cookie, a classic gateau, a dark truffle, and a spicy hot chocolate, all of them featured in the following pages. In 85 recipes, by eight top chefs, 'I Love Chocolate' contains a heavenly selection of creations, for every occasion.

The great surprise about chocolate we enjoy today is that it was ever invented. It comes from the bean inside the cocoa pod, a fruit that grows directly on the trunk of the tree. Yet the bean needs to go through many stages of processing before it becomes the bar or callet which forms the basis of all the recipes here. It has taken centuries of development to learn how to release the several hundred flavours in cocoa and develop the silky feel. Fermenting and roasting, winnowing and conching are all essential processes in the journey from the bean to the bar, and each has to be managed correctly to ensure a perfect finish.

To the Olmecs, the Maya and the Aztecs in Central America, chocolate was a divine gift which they served as a drink (though admittedly it would have been rather thin and unpleasant to our taste). As a drink is how it was first enjoyed when it was brought to Europe. Gradually chefs started to experiment and learned to add the sweet spices, the sugar and the cream or butter that we have come to expect in our chocolate.

Of course, there's no one type of chocolate. The cook and chef today can vary the recipe depending on the chocolate chosen. Cocoa is grown around the world – from Central America to Africa, to Indonesia and Vietnam – and in every origin the flavours are subtly different. Sometimes a blend will be perfect for the recipe, at others a 'single origin chocolate' works best. The choice is yours, and the variety is enormous. The only way to find the right one is to start experimenting.

Before you start cooking, read the section on tempering and pre-crystallising chocolate and on making ganaches (p16-20). Master these techniques to guarantee a professional finish. All the recipes here have been contributed by Master Chocolatiers, award-winning chefs, and experienced trainers. Their recipes are tried and tested and are guaranteed to bring you pleasure and praise, time and again.

The recipes in this book have been created using specific chocolate products, and whilst other brands can be used it is recommended that when following the recipes you use the chocolate as described in the recipe to ensure the best result.

All the chocolate is available from www.ilovechoc.net as listed on page 21.

3

BEVERLEY DUNKLEY

BEVERLEY DUNKLEY IS HEAD OF THE UK CHOCOLATE ACADEMY AT BARRY CALLEBAUT IN BANBURY, OXFORDSHIRE, AND TEACHES CHOCOLATIERS AT ALL LEVELS FROM THE HOME HOBBY CHOCOLATE LOVER TO THE FINEST CHOCOLATE SCULPTORS AND PASTRY CHEFS.

Beverley has a real passion for patisserie and chocolate work.

In her early career she moved to Switzerland to work in the Sugar School of world-renowned pastry chef Ewald Notter, then she worked with Relais Desserts in Luxembourg where first-hand experience was gained in the production of French and German patisserie. She later became a lecturer in Patisserie at Morecambe College of Further Education teaching 16-19 year olds Baking skills and the art of Patisserie. She joined Barry Callebaut in 1995 and was initially responsible for the management of direct chocolate and distributor accounts in the South of England.

Beverley has been in demand as a judge at the SBST Bakery Student Awards, Hotelympia, the UK Chocolate Masters, and has helped organise the Junior UK Chocolate Masters.

Beverley is committed to helping people learn new chocolate skills and develop their careers and she loves to promote a desire to work with chocolate.

In her own words "Chocolate is fun to eat and work with and I hope you enjoy making and eating the recipes I have prepared for you in this book."

www.chocolate-academy.com

4

DIRK SCHONKEREN

DIRK SCHONKEREN IS A CHEF AND MASTER CHOCOLATIER WITH 40 YEARS EXPERIENCE. AS A YOUNG BOY HE WORKED IN LOCAL RESTAURANTS AND IN HIS MOTHER'S DELICATESSEN AND GRADUATED FROM THE PRESTIGIOUS PIVA COLLEGE IN ANTWERP, BELGIUM. DIRK HELD NUMEROUS POSITIONS AS CHEF DE PARTIE AND AS A PASTRY CHEF IN RESTAURANTS AND HOTELS IN ANTWERP AND BRUSSELS.

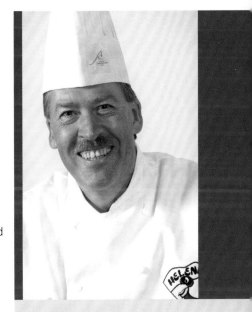

With his Irish wife Elaine O'Mahony, he moved to Ireland to take up the position of Culinary Arts lecturer in Rockwell College.

Dirk also worked as executive head chef in some of Ireland's top hotels and in 1983 won the National Dairy Council "Irish Cheese Board and Cheese Recipe" competition.

Together with his wife Elaine he set up an artisan chocolaterie and named it Helena Chocolates, supplying restaurants, hotels and speciality shops with beautiful chocolate creations. They opened their first chocolate shop in Castlebar, Co. Mayo in 1988 and a second shop in Galway in 1992.

Dirk was a finalist in the UK Chocolate Masters in 2006, and in 2007 Helena Chocolates moved to larger premises and opened a chocolate shop with a restaurant and dessert lounge.

In 2009 Dirk was invited to join the Callebaut Ambassador's Club as their first Irish ambassador.

As well as managing a busy chocolate shop and restaurant, Dirk still finds the time to make exquisite chocolate sculptures, creating gastronomic dishes with chocolate as well as continuing to teach the arts of chocolate and pastry.

www.dumouchel.co.uk

IAIN BURNETT

IAIN BURNETT HIGHLAND CHOCOLATIER

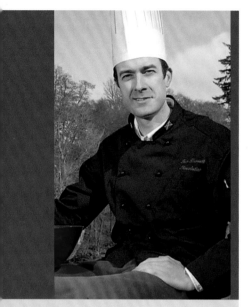

WORLD CLASS CHOCOLATIER IAIN BURNETT HIGHLAND CHOCOLATIER HAS BECOME INTERNATIONALLY RECOGNISED AS A MASTER TRUFFLE SPECIALIST. HIS OUTSTANDING CHOCOLATES HAVE GARNERED THE CHOCOLATE WORLD'S HIGHEST ACCOLADES: SWEEPING GOLD, SILVER AND BRONZE FROM THE ACADEMY OF CHOCOLATE; TRIPLE GOLD STARS IN THE NATIONAL GREAT TASTE AWARDS; AND TWICE EXCELLENCE AWARDS FROM SCOTLAND FOOD AND DRINK.

From his bespoke chocolate kitchen near Pitlochry in Highland Perthshire, Iain Burnett Highland Chocolatier creates chocolates of an unparalleled quality for a selection of high profile gourmet chefs and retailers. Clients include 5 star hotels, Michelin star restaurants and prestigious venues throughout the world. Iain's website expresses his passion, which is also clearly apparent to those who have visited his award-winning tourist attraction The Scottish Chocolate Centre.

Iain learned his initial culinary skills from his father who trained him from a young age to select from amongst the best of Scottish ingredients and exotic spices to create new flavours and textures. His passion for chocolate began in Japan upon discovering a Maître Chocolatier there who had created an exceptional truffle using only natural ingredients.

Iain's training under Master Chocolatiers of the Belgian, Swiss and French schools led to the creation of his own renowned collection of Velvet Truffles™ and Spiced Pralines. His Velvet Truffles™ are testimony to the virtues of patience and excellence plus high quality single-origin cocoa and fresh local Scottish cream. Iain and his team's pièce de résistance is the Cocoa Dusted Velvet Truffle™ – exquisite and unique in the breadth of its flavour profile and silky texture. It is served "naked", rather than enrobed in a hard chocolate shell, as a petit four with a truffle fork.

Iain dedicated more than 3 years to the refinement of his signature Velvet Truffle™ method and in the process developed what is required to be a genuine artisan chocolatier.

www.HighlandChocolatier.com

6

JOHN HUBER

WIDELY KNOWN AS THE KING OF PASTRY AND ONE OF THE UK'S MOST INFLUENTIAL PASTRY CHEFS, THE LATE JOHN HUBER WAS BORN IN SWITZERLAND BUT REGARDED ENGLAND AS HIS ADOPTED COUNTRY. HIS CONTRIBUTION TO FINE PASTRY WORK IN THE UK WAS PART OF A LENGTHY AND DISTINGUISHED CAREER STARTING IN 1967 WHEN HE JOINED SLOUGH COLLEGE OF HIGHER EDUCATION AS A LECTURER.

The department he joined was then known as the department of domestic science, art, hairdressing, pottery and catering, with catering being regarded as the poor relation.

Undeterred, Huber put together the first two-year day-release pastry course which culminated in a six hour practical examination, by using as a role model, the Swiss National Diploma for pâtissiers, confisseurs and glaciers, a diploma for which he himself had studied. Backed by the City & Guilds, the first students joined the course in 1972 and this was to form the basis of two advanced pastry courses which were to remain the mainstay of pastry education in the UK. He then spent over 30 years at Thames Valley University, where he transformed forever the way pastry was taught in the UK. His achievements were recognised in 1995 when he was invested as a Professor of Pastry, becoming the first pastry chef to be awarded the honour in the UK.

As well as being a pioneer in pastry education, John was equally well known in the industry for his enormous skill, enthusiasm and tireless energy. His teaching saw many of his students gain key roles in some of the best hotels and restaurants.

Huber recognised the need to continuously learn and was as enthusiastic as any of the students he taught in expanding his skills. He would regularly use a summer vacation to go to the continent to study saying "You are never too old to learn; I was in my 50's and was the oldest stagière they'd ever had!"

John's legacy to pastry education and the development of pastry in this country lives on and we hope that you enjoy preparing and eating his chocolate recipes included in this book.

JOHN SLATTERY

Having worked in baking and confectionery all his life, and being part of the family business for over 40 years, spending every day with his favourite ingredient was a natural move for John. After training at college, John attended courses in the chocolate capitals of the world; Switzerland, Belgium and Austria among others, gaining both skills and experience. His passion for chocolate is clear, as John is a member of the British Confectioners Association, The National Association of Master Bakers and the International Richemont Club – a centre for master bakers and confectioners.

Now John shares his love of chocolate with others, in the form of Slattery Pâtissier & Chocolatier Ltd, a three storey chocolate shop based on Bury New Road in Whitefield, Manchester. Affectionately known as 'That wicked shop', this unique store specialises in celebration cakes and chocolate treats, and prides itself on being able to create anything in chocolate! Of course, hand-made chocolates and chocolate gifts are also available, plus a dining room above, offering breakfast, lunch and afternoon tea.

John also offers a variety of courses in chocolate, cake decorating and other confectionery on the third floor of the shop, otherwise known as The School of Excellence. It is here that he and his staff meet many chocolate lovers who wish to advance their skills.

John has written two books, *'Chocolate Unwrapped'* and *'John Slattery's Creative Chocolate'* and he says with a smile, "After all, the art of chocolate doesn't need to be just for experts."

Unwrap your chocolate potential with John's inspirational and delicious recipes and give in to your own love of chocolate with *'I Love Chocolate'*.

JOHN SLATTERY HAS ALWAYS BEEN A LITTLE IN LOVE WITH CHOCOLATE – EATING IT, COOKING WITH IT, CREATING WITH IT – FOR JOHN, CHOCOLATE CAN BE USED TO CREATE A MILLION POSSIBILITIES.

www.slattery.co.uk

8

MARK TILLING

MARK TILLING HAS BEEN WORKING FOR OVER 20 YEARS IN THE PATISSERIE AND CHOCOLATE WORLD FOR WHICH HE HAS A GREAT PASSION. HE STARTED WORKING IN A HOTEL AT WEEKENDS BEFORE HE LEFT SCHOOL AND HAS WORKED IN MANY DIFFERENT HOTELS AND RESTAURANTS AROUND THE UK INCLUDING THE LANESBOROUGH ON HYDE PARK, LAINSTON HOUSE HOTEL IN WINCHESTER, HOTEL DU VIN WINCHESTER AND BRISTOL AND LE PAVE D'AUGE IN NORMANDY, FRANCE, WHICH BOASTS A MICHELIN STAR.

Mark has received many awards for his chocolate and patisserie work over the years. He has earned many gold and silver medals in desserts and petits fours as well as double gold in chocolate showpieces. His biggest achievement was twice winning the UK Chocolate Masters over a four year period from 2006-2010. He then represented the UK in the finals of the World Chocolate Masters in 2007 and 2009 coming 12th in 2007 and 7th in 2009. Coming 7th was the highest-ever UK placing and a great honour.

Now he teaches at Squires Kitchen International School in Farnham, Surrey, providing courses in chocolate and patisserie including five day chocolate schools, macaroon days and French patisserie classes. Mark says, "It's a great pleasure teaching and passing on my knowledge to everyone who comes to Squires."

Mark has written two books for Squires Kitchen *'Working with Chocolate'* and *'Making Macaroons'* and will soon be publishing a third book on chocolate wedding cakes and all sweet things.

Mark has used Thermomix for his competition work and teaching for many years and comments, " Thermomix, the best machine on the market – what can it not do! I couldn't have been without it at the World Chocolate Masters 2009. Thermomix takes competition work to the next level, I love it!"

www.squires-school.co.uk

9

RUTH HINKS

AS THE CURRENT HOLDER OF THE PRESTIGIOUS 'UK CHOCOLATE MASTER' TITLE, RUTH HAS WORKED AS A PROFESSIONAL CHOCOLATIER AND PASTRY CHEF FOR OVER TWO DECADES. HER PASSION FOR COMPETITION AND DESIRE TO WORK WITH THE VERY BEST IN THE INDUSTRY HAS BROUGHT HER WIDESPREAD ACCLAIM AND RECOGNITION. PRIOR TO BECOMING THE UK CHOCOLATE MASTER, RUTH WAS ALSO NAMED UK CONFECTIONER OF THE YEAR 2011, AUSTRALIAN PASTRY CHEF OF THE YEAR AND WON GOLD AND SILVER MEDALS AT THE CULINARY OLYMPICS IN 2000 AND 2004.

Prior to launching Cocoa Black, Ruth held Head Pastry Chef positions with numerous 5-star hotels, most recently the Sheraton Grand Hotel in Edinburgh. She trained at the Cocoa Barry Chocolate School in Paris and the Carma Chocolate Academy in Switzerland. Ruth's love for chocolate started aged 14 when as a schoolgirl she would make and sell handmade Easter eggs to raise pocket money.

As a founder and director of the chocolate manufacturer Cocoa Black, Ruth is now spending as much time in the boardroom and at international demonstrations as she does in her production kitchen. With the launch of the Cocoa Black Chocolate & Pastry School in Peebles, near Edinburgh, Ruth now creates and delivers chocolate and pastry training for professional and domestic cooks. The Cocoa Black shop and café has grown rapidly, as has interest in the company's website which is now receiving orders from all over the world.

www.cocoablack.com

THIERRY DUMOUCHEL

BORN AND RAISED IN RURAL NORMANDY, FROM A VERY YOUNG AGE THIERRY LEARNED TO APPRECIATE THE VALUE OF FRESH, QUALITY FOOD. AS PART OF A FARMING FAMILY, HE TOOK PART IN THE GROWING AND REARING OF THE FOOD THEY ATE AND IS A GREAT BELIEVER IN THE SAYING 'YOU ARE WHAT YOU EAT!' THIERRY HAS ALWAYS BEEN AGAINST THE ADDITION OF ANY ARTIFICIAL CHEMICALS AND PRESERVATIVES TO THE FOOD WE CONSUME. IT IS THIS PHILOSOPHY THAT INSPIRES HIM TO CREATE THE BREADS, CAKES AND PASTRIES WHICH MAKES DUMOUCHEL SO SPECIAL.

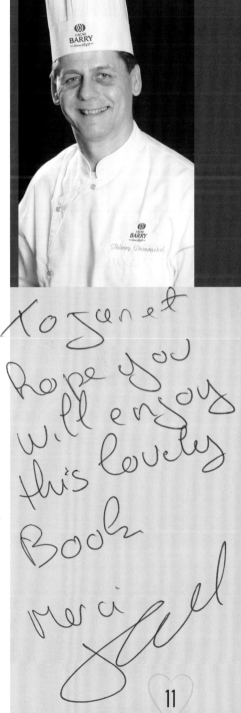

Thierry Dumouchel trained at the renowned food college in Rouen, France, and worked in Paris, London, Sydney and Tokyo before opening his patisserie in 1998 in Yorkshire. As a master of his craft and as UK ambassador for Barry Callebaut and the world renowned Cointreau, Thierry is often called upon to do demonstrations. He also works as a consultant offering advice and guidance to individuals and businesses around the UK and has been technical director and senior lecturer for the world famous Le Cordon Bleu Organisation.

In 2012, Dumouchel patisserie was extremely proud to have won The Baking Industry "Craft Business Award". The same year also saw the launch of Thierry's online artisan bread. The freshly baked bread is delivered by courier, lightly baked, bagged and ready to freeze. Simply defrost, finish in the oven and enjoy!

"Baking and chocolate are things to be savoured and definitely not rushed. All our breads, cakes and chocolate creations are made very naturally. We simply use good ingredients, and we don't add chemicals. Ever! This produces flavour and quality. We simply refuse to compromise." Thierry's recipes reflect this approach and we hope you enjoy them!

www.dumouchel.co.uk

11

"MAN CANNOT LIVE ON CHOCOLATE ALONE; BUT WOMAN SURE CAN."

ANON

CONTENTS

UNDERSTANDING TEMPERING

CHOCOLATE IS ONE OF THE MOST WONDERFUL COMMODITIES TO WORK WITH. THE WAY IT LOOKS, FEELS AND OF COURSE, TASTES IS EXQUISITE. HOWEVER IT IS IMPORTANT TO HAVE A KNOWLEDGE AND UNDERSTANDING OF ITS COMPLEXITIES IF YOU ARE TO HAVE CONSISTENTLY SUCCESSFUL EXPERIENCES WHEN WORKING WITH IT.

Chocolate's only limits are your own imagination!

Tempering chocolate is an important process for a number of reasons, including the look and taste of the finished product, as it determines the amount and quality of pre-crystallising achieved from the cocoa butter present in the chocolate.

This, in turn, is dependent on the cocoa butter content of the chocolate, and how it works within the chocolate. Cocoa butter is the fat of the cocoa bean, and it is the presence of the cocoa butter that:

- ✕ **Creates chocolate with a good gloss/shine**
- ✕ **Allows chocolate to release from moulds as it contracts**
- ✕ **Has a sensational mouth feel, melting in the mouth**
- ✕ **Gives the chocolate a hardness which clearly snaps when broken**

However it is the same cocoa butter that can:

- ✕ **Give chocolate white streaks over its surface (fat bloom)**
- ✕ **Cause it to melt very quickly when touched**
- ✕ **Make it feel grainy on the tongue (sugar bloom)**
- ✕ **Cause it to bend, then break without its characteristic snap**

SO HOW IS THIS POSSIBLE?

The reasons for this very special ingredient behaving so very differently is because it is polymorphic, which means it can change depending on its circumstances at the time.

Chocolatiers now know that it's not just the temperature of the chocolate that matters, but also the crystal formation at the time of preparation and manufacture. Cocoa butter is thought to contain six different crystals and it can adapt from one to another depending on the varying amounts of time, temperature and movement, given to the chocolate.

Unfortunately not all of these six crystals are of a stable structure and don't lock together when set, and only stable crystals will ensure all the good qualities of chocolate.

Previously, it was thought that these crystals, in body temperature chocolate, were stable and would give the correct formation when set. However, we now know that if chocolate does not receive any or sufficient movement when being melted, there will be insufficient crystals present to allow the characteristics of the cocoa butter to be realised – meaning no snap, graininess, etc.

Pre-crystallising of the chocolate requires:
- ✕ **TIME**
- ✕ **TEMPERATURE**
- ✕ **MOVEMENT**
- ✕ **TEST**

These four things will help to ensure your chocolate is perfect each and every time.

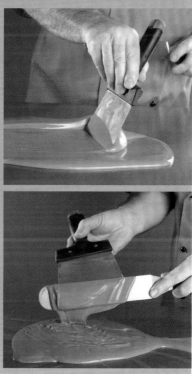

EQUIPMENT:

Plastic mixing bowl
Spoon
heat source (bain-marie
  or microwave)

MELTING CHOCOLATE

Good quality chocolate contains cocoa butter and melts at a temperature just below our own body temperature.

It is therefore important not to over heat chocolate as it will burn easily. Remember, as chocolate melts at body temperature, there is no need to place it over direct heat to melt it. Chocolate melts easily when placed into an electric or manual hot water Bain-Marie, or in the low dry heat of a microwave. If you melt chocolate over warm water, take care not to get water into the chocolate. Even in the form of steam/vapour coming from the pan as this moisture will thicken the

chocolate making it difficult to work with. If you want to work using this method, wrap a tea towel around the base of the bowl with the chocolate in it, to prevent vapour rising from the pan.

MILK AND WHITE CHOCOLATE:

The methods given to pre-crystallise chocolate are the same for white, milk and dark varieties. However, due to the additional milk and sugar content of milk and white chocolate, **extra care is needed during the melting process** to ensure the chocolate does not burn and therefore become grainy and unusable.

PRE-CRYSTALLISING CHOCOLATE

EQUIPMENT:

Plastic mixing bowl
Spoon
Heat source (bain-marie or microwave)
Marble work top
Scraper
Step pallet knife

PRE-CRYSTALLISING TIP:
CHOCOLATE CAN BE PRE-CRYSTALLISED IN MANY WAYS. CHOOSE THE WAY THAT SUITS YOU. AS LONG AS THE PRINCIPLES OF CREATING STABLE CRYSTALS ARE ADHERED TO IT'S WHATEVER WORKS FOR YOU.

TABLE METHODS:

Completely melt the chocolate in the microwave or electric bain-marie. The chocolate will look very fluid, and will therefore have no crystals within it. Used in this condition the end product will be of poor quality.

Stable crystals now have to be produced, this is quite simple as the chocolate has already been given the time and temperature to melt. We now have to move the chocolate to create the stable crystals. Only a relatively small proportion of crystals are required, so pour approximately two-thirds of the liquid chocolate on to a clean dry surface such as marble, granite or stainless steel. Working the chocolate backwards and forwards with a scraper, as it thickens, forms the stable crystals.

Before it sets, place this chocolate back into the warmer chocolate and stir well. The warmer chocolate will help bring a nice fluidity back to the chocolate, and the worked chocolate will have enough stable crystals to give some to the unworked chocolate. Once mixed together, the chocolate can be tested to make sure it has stable crystals within it and will therefore produce good quality products.

SEEDING METHOD:

The seeding method is very similar to the table method in that the chocolate is fully melted. However instead of pouring the chocolate onto the table, additional chocolate pieces/buttons can be stirred into the warm chocolate. Adding the buttons to 'seed' the warm, liquid chocolate makes sense as it introduces the movement required to pre-crystallise the chocolate. This is less messy as it can be done in a bain-marie. The amount of pieces/buttons will depend on the type of chocolate and how much the chocolate is moved. Test the chocolate before using.

MICROWAVE METHOD:

The microwave method is the fasted way to pre-crystallise your chocolate and very inexpensive. Depending on the size of the bowl of chocolate, place into a microwave for 1 minute for a large bowl or 30 seconds if small. Place on full power (up to 1000W) and then remove from the microwave.

Stir and, if less than two-thirds of the chocolate pieces have melted, then return to microwave. Be flexible, it may be nearly there and only need another 30 seconds, or even 10 seconds, it is important that there are around one third of the buttons left unmelted for this method to work.

Once two-thirds of the chocolate has melted, use a heat gun or hairdryer to help the remaining buttons melt. These will seed the liquid chocolate and, when all the buttons have disappeared, do the following test to ensure you have a stable structure to your chocolate.

TESTING THE CHOCOLATE

EQUIPMENT:
Scraper, step-palette knife
  or knife
Clock/timer
Heat gun/hair dryer

PRE-CRYSTALLISING TIP:
CHOCOLATIERS ARE OFTEN TOLD TO TAKE A SAMPLE OR TEST AND WAIT JUST 3 MINUTES. THIS IS OK, BUT IT CAN BE BETTER FOR THE CHOCOLATE TO BE A LITTLE MORE FLUID WHEN YOU ARE LEARNING, AS THIS GIVES YOU MORE TIME WHEN PROCESSING THE CHOCOLATE INTO MOULDS BUT STILL RETAINS THE CORRECT AMOUNT OF CRYSTALS, TO GIVE GOOD RESULTS.

THE ALL IMPORTANT TEST:

The test is the most important thing you can do when determining if chocolate is ready as this will tell you, before you start using the chocolate, how your products will look.

Simply dip the scraper or palette knife part-way into the chocolate, scrape one side clean on the bowl edge and leave for 5 minutes. The chocolate in the bowl will be completely fine for this 5 minute period.

CHOCOLATE HAS 3 STAGES IN ITS PROCESS:

1. **MELTED:** chocolate will be fluid
2. **TOUCH DRY:** Chocolate becomes touch dry when left to dry
3. **COMPLETELY DRY:** Chocolate contracts, and it is completely dry

If the sample chocolate is touch dry in the 5 minute period, your chocolate has the correct amount of crystals to ensure you will have the perfect chocolate. However, if the chocolate is still fluid after 5 minutes, you have some stable crystals but not enough to give the chocolate a good gloss and snap when eaten.

To combat this you can either pour a little on the table and move the chocolate to create some extra crystals or add some more buttons to the liquid chocolate. Either way will increase the amount of crystals. Redo the test to check.

If, however, the opposite occurs and the chocolate sets in under 5 minutes, this means that you have good stable crystals, but too many. Having too many might sound like a good thing but it will make the chocolate thick and very hard to work with.

In this case, all that is required is a little heat from the heat gun or hair dryer to reduce the amount of crystals, then redo the test. However, it is important to note that, as with all methods of pre-crystallising, chocolate has to remain in a good crystalline form throughout the manufacture of your items. **When using the heat gun or hair dryer on chocolate, which has no thermostat to control the heat, it is important to take great care.** It's also worth remembering that while working with the chocolate you are creating movement, which is one of the factors needed to create stable crystals. Therefore it's quite possible for the chocolate to become thick while working with it. This is easily solved by using the heat gun/hair dryer again: little and often to keep the chocolate at its optimum crystalline state.

GANACHE FOR POURING OR FILLING

	Dark Chocolate 54%	Milk Chocolate 33%	White Chocolate 26%
Whipping Cream	125g	125g	125g
Glucose	30g	30g	30g
Chocolate	175g	250g	300g
Total Weight	330g	405g	455g

METHOD:

1. Bring the cream and glucose to the boil and pour over the chocolate buttons/pieces. Wait a few moments to allow the heat of the cream to warm through the buttons/pieces. Stir well to create a smooth emulsion. As the ganache cools it will become thicker – pour over the cake while still warm and runny, but not hot.

2. Alternatively you can heat the cream and glucose and mix with melted tempered chocolate. Stir well and pour over the cake when the correct viscosity is reached.

3. If you wish to use this recipe for the filling in a cake, seal in airtight container and allow to stand at room temperature overnight. When you wish to use the ganache, put it in a machine bowl with a beater and mix on medium speed until a lighter consistency suitable for spreading is achieved.

Working with Chocolate reproduced by kind permission from Creative Chocolate by John Slattery

20

I ♥ CHOCOLATE
BUYING CHOCOLATE

All the recipes in this book have been tested with Callebaut chocolate containing only cocoa butter i.e. no vegetable oils or fats. We recommend using the Callebaut brand whenever possible in order to get excellent results. To make it easy for you to buy Callebaut chocolate, our website www.ilovechoc.net links to an online shop where you can purchase this high quality chocolate in small and large quantities.

These are the Callebaut chocolates we have used in our recipes:

Callebaut 70-30-38 dark chocolate 70%	300g	1kg	5kg
Callebaut 811 NV dark chocolate 54%	300g	1kg	5kg
Callebaut 823 NV milk chocolate 33%	300g	1kg	5kg
Callebaut W2 NV white chocolate	300g	1kg	5kg
Callebaut caramel flavoured chocolate	300g		

You may also like to try using single origin chocolate.

Callebaut Origin chocolates, also available via www.ilovechoc.net, include the following and others may be available on request:

Java milk chocolate 32%
Ecuador dark chocolate 70%
Grenade dark chocolate 60%
Saothome dark chocolate 70%
Madagascar dark chocolate 67%

www.ilovechoc.net

21

CAKES

CHOCOLATE AND
PEANUT BUTTER CUP CAKES

MAKES 12 CUP CAKES

ingredients

125g Unsalted butter
125g Soft brown sugar
2 Large eggs
40ml Buttermilk
100g Self-raising flour
25g Cocoa powder
25g Salted peanuts, crushed into
   small pieces
35g Chocolate chips

BUTTERCREAM FILLING:

315g Chunky peanut butter
195g Icing sugar
225g Unsalted butter

method

1. Preheat the oven to 160°C.
2. Cream the butter and sugar together until light and fluffy.
3. Add the eggs one at a time and then the buttermilk until all incorporated.
4. Sieve the flour and cocoa powder together and fold into the mix.
5. Finally fold in the peanuts and chocolate chips and, using a piping bag or teaspoon, pipe or spoon the mixture into cup cake cases that are already lined in a muffin tin and fill to three-quarters full.
6. Bake in the oven for 20-25 minutes or until cooked.

FILLING:

1. Place the peanut butter, icing sugar and butter in a mixer with a beater and mix until light and fluffy.
2. When the cup cakes are cooled pipe or spoon on the buttercream filling and garnish with decorations of your choice.

24

CHOCOLATE AND
BLUEBERRY MUFFINS

CHOCOLATE AND
BLUEBERRY MUFFINS

FOR ABOUT 15 LARGE MUFFINS

ingredients

650g Plain white flour
225g Icing sugar
15g Baking powder
1 Pinch salt
5 Whole free-range eggs
600ml Full-fat milk
250g Butter
150g Vegetable oil
300g Chocolate chunks
300g Fresh or frozen blueberries

TO FINISH:

100ml Single cream
120g Callebaut 811 NV, 54% dark
   chocolate,
White chocolate vermicelli, white
   marshmallows or fresh blueberries,
   to decorate

method

1. Take three large bowls and a whisk. In bowl one mix the dry ingredients together. In bowl two whisk up the eggs until frothy and then add the milk. Put the butter in the third bowl, place in a microwave oven until melted, then add the vegetable oil.
2. Using the whisk, pour the egg and milk mixture into the dry ingredients until smooth, then add the butter and oil mixture. Allow to stand for 5 minutes, then pour the dough into muffin cases. Add to each case some chocolate chunks and blueberries and with a spoon push them under the surface of the dough.
3. Bake the muffins at 180°C for about 25 minutes. Check by inserting a skewer into the muffins – if it comes out clean, the muffins are cooked through. Allow to cool.

TO FINISH:

1. Heat the cream in a microwave then stir in the dark chocolate. Whisk until smooth.
2. Spoon some of this glaze on top of the muffin and decorate with white vermicelli, white marshmallows or fresh blueberries as desired.

FRUIT AND
NUT TIFFIN

MAKES 16

ingredients

125g Golden syrup
125g Caramel
250g Unsalted butter
750g Digestive biscuit crumbs
100g Sultanas
100g Raisins
100g Glacé cherries
50g Walnut halves
50g Pecan halves
50g Roasted hazelnuts
25g Brazil nuts chopped
500g Callebaut dark chocolate 70% ,
   melted

method

1.   Warm together the syrup, caramel and butter.
2.   Add to the digestive crumbs and part mix.
3.   Add all the fruit and nuts and part mix again.
4.   Add the melted chocolate and mix completely together.
5.   Pour onto a greaseproof paper lined tray, 76x46cm.
6.   Allow to set in the fridge until firm.
7.   Cut into fingers or squares.
8.   Squares can be coated on the base with chocolate, fully enrobed or just spun with chocolate to decorate as desired.

CHEF'S TIP

This recipe keeps well and is versatile as it can be presented as a cake slice finger. Cut small it makes a good 'mini bite' or cut even smaller it can make a great addition to your petit four

DARK TRUFFLE GANACHE CAKE

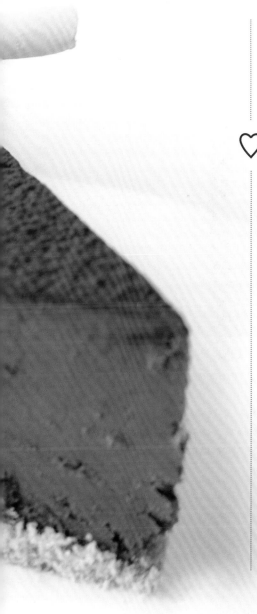

ingredients

75g Amaretti biscuits, crushed
440g 70% Venezuela Amedei Chuao dark chocolate
50g 33% Madagascar Tanariva milk chocolate
5 tbsp Liquid glucose
570ml Double cream

TO SERVE:

Cocoa powder for dusting
Single cream, to serve (optional)

method

1. Line a 23cm cake tin with greaseproof or silicone paper and brush the base and sides lightly with oil.
2. Sprinkle the crushed Amaretti over the base of the tin. These can be worked with a very little butter if a firmer base is preferred.
3. Melt the chocolates and glucose in a heat-proof bowl over a pan of simmering water. Leave to cool for five minutes until warm.
4. Beat the cream until slightly thick. Fold half into the chocolate mixture, then fold that mixture into the rest of the cream.
5. Spoon the smoothly blended mixture into the prepared tin. Tap the tin gently to even the mixture out. Cover with cling film and chill overnight.
6. Just before serving run a palette knife round the edge to loosen then give it a good shake and turn out onto a serving plate.
7. Dust the surface with sifted cocoa powder.

CHOCOLATE SIMNEL CAKE

CHOCOLATE SIMNEL CAKE

SERVES 12

ingredients

SIMNEL CAKE:

150g Chopped candied fruit
150g Currants
1 tsp Grated lemon zest
1 tsp Vanilla extract
2 tbsp Brandy
3 Eggs
100g Caster sugar
50g Callebaut 811NV dark chocolate
50g Unsalted butter
110g Plain flour
15g Cacao Barry Extra Brute
    Cocoa Powder
150g White marzipan

DECORATION:

150g Callebaut 811NV dark chocolate
150g Double cream
Small easter eggs

NEST DECORATION:

Callebaut 811NV dark chocolate
Callebaut W2NV white chocolate
Moulded chocolate hen

method

SIMNEL CAKE:

1. Preheat the oven to 180°C.
2. Line an 18cm round deep cake tin with silicone paper.
3. Put the fruit and lemon zest into a bowl.
4. Pour over the vanilla extract and brandy, then allow to stand for at least 20 minutes.
5. Cream the eggs and sugar with the aid of an electric mixer.
6. Melt together the dark chocolate and butter, then cool to body temperature.
7. Stir the sieved flour and cocoa powder into the creamed eggs and sugar batter.
8. Gently stir in the melted chocolate and butter.
9. Lastly stir in the soaked fruits.
10. Pour half the batter into the prepared cake tin.
11. Roll the marzipan into a disc about 15x1cm in thickness and place on top of the cake batter.
12. Cover completely with the remaining batter.
13. Bake for approximately 50 minutes.

DECORATION:

1. Put the chocolate and cream into a bowl.
2. Cook for 1 minute in a microwave at full power.
3. Stir well to create a smooth glaze.
4. Spread half the glaze on top of the cake with a palette knife, allowing the glaze to pour off the sides slightly.
5. Aerate the rest of the glaze slightly with a balloon whisk.
6. Pipe 11 rosettes around the top of the cake, placing a small easter egg on each.

NEST DECORATION:

1. Melt the chocolates separately and place into separate paper cones.
2. Pipe fine long lines of white chocolate onto a frozen granite tile.
3. Pipe long lines of dark chocolate on top of the white chocolate; the chocolate does not have to be tempered for this application. The chocolate will set immediately on the frozen granite, but remain flexible.
4. Lift the chocolate lines with a palette knife and wrap around the cake to make the chocolate nest.
5. Decorate the centre of the cake with a moulded chocolate hen.

"IT'S NOT THAT CHOCOLATES
ARE A SUBSTITUTE FOR LOVE.
LOVE IS A SUBSTITUTE
FOR CHOCOLATE.
CHOCOLATE IS, LET'S FACE IT,
FAR MORE RELIABLE THAN
A MAN."

MIRANDA INGRAM

38

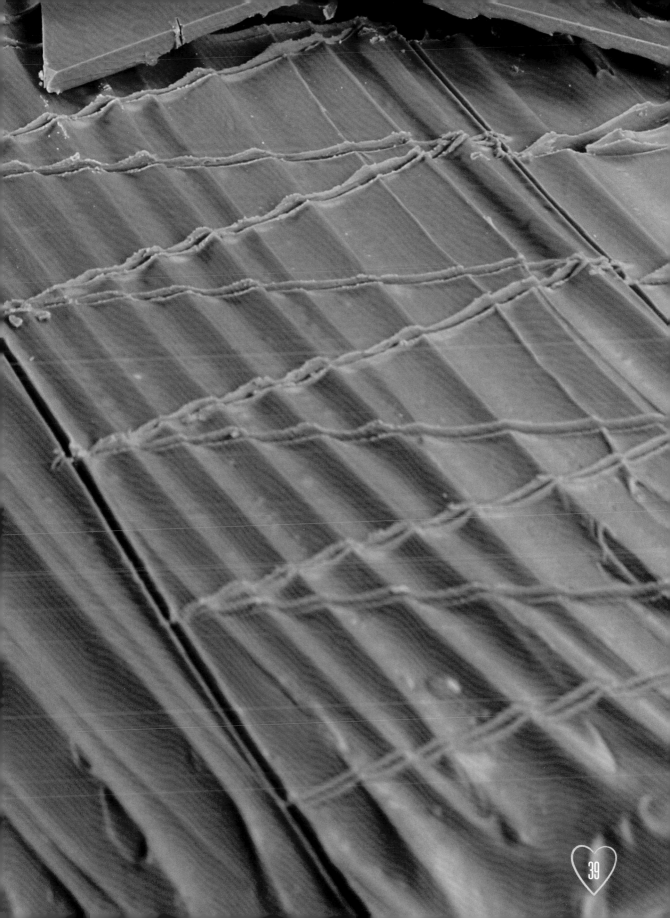

CHOCOLATE MUFFINS

MAKES 10-12 MUFFINS

ingredients

100g Unsalted butter
250g Soft brown sugar
2 Large eggs
150ml Sour cream
200g Plain flour
50g Brown flour
1 tsp Bicarbonate of soda
2 tbsp Cocoa powder
200g Callebaut 811 NV, 54% dark
    chocolate, chopped into small
    pieces

method

1. Preheat the oven to 170°C.
2. Cream the butter and sugar together until light and fluffy, then add the eggs one at a time until all incorporated.
3. Pour in the cream and mix until also incorporated.
4. Sieve the flours, bicarbonate of soda and cocoa powder together and fold into the mix.
5. Fold in the chocolate.
6. Cut some baking paper into 15cm squares and push each one into the cavities of a cup cake pan so the sides rise above to make homemade cup cake cases.
7. Spoon in the mix to about halfway full and bake for 25 minutes or until cooked – springy to the touch.
8. Decorate with chocolate ganache and gold colour dusted, chocolate coated popping candy.

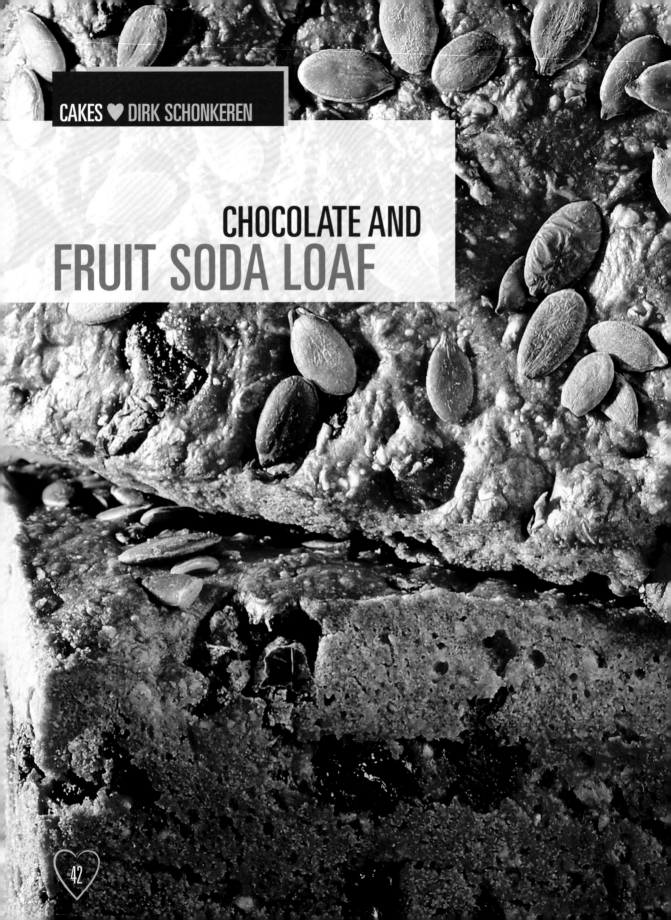

CAKES ♥ DIRK SCHONKEREN

CHOCOLATE AND
FRUIT SODA LOAF

CHOCOLATE AND
FRUIT SODA LOAF

MAKES 3 LOAVES USING A TIN APPROXIMATELY 21 X 11 X 6CM DEEP

ingredients

40g Dried apricots, halved
40g Sultanas
40g Glace cherries
40g Dates
20g Goji berries
50g Brown sugar
125g Callebaut dark bake-stable
   chocolate chunks
120g Bran
50g Porridge oats
50g Wheat germ
350g Plain white flour
270g Wholemeal flour
20g Baking powder
7g Bicarbonate of soda
10g Sea salt
2 Large free-range eggs
50g Honey
1 litre Buttermilk
25g Pumpkin seeds

TO SERVE:

Butter or chocolate spread
   (see p217 for recipe)

method

1. Mix all the fruit, brown sugar and chocolate chunks together with all the other dry ingredients in a large bowl.
2. Whisk the eggs, honey and buttermilk together and pour over the fruit and other dry ingredients.
3. Mix well using a wooden spoon and fill the greased and floured baking tins with the mixture.
4. Sprinkle the top with the pumpkin seeds and bake at 160°C for 65 minutes. Take out of the tins and allow to cool on a cooling rack.

TO SERVE:

1. Serve with butter or chocolate spread.

SACHER TORTE

1 X 20CM CAKE RING

ingredients

SPONGE:

150g Callebaut 811 NV, 54% dark
   chocolate
145g Unsalted butter
70g Caster sugar
145g Egg yolks
220g Egg whites
60g Caster sugar
70g Flour
4g Baking powder
150g Ground almonds

GANACHE:

300g Cream
60g Glucose
60g Sugar
300g Callebaut 811 NV, 54% dark
   chocolate
60g Butter

ASSEMBLY:

Apricot jam for masking

method

SPONGE:

1. Melt the dark chocolate.
2. Cream the butter and 70g of caster sugar until light and fluffy.
3. Add in the egg yolks and beat well.
4. Whisk up the whites and 60g of caster sugar to soft peaks.
5. Fold the flour, baking powder and ground almonds into the chocolate mixture.
6. Then fold in the egg whites.
7. Bake at 180°C for about 30–40 minutes.
8. Allow to cool, cut it in half and sandwich together with apricot jam.
9. Mask the cake with apricot jam and then glaze with ganache.

GANACHE:

1. Bring to the boil the cream, glucose and sugar.
2. Pour over the chopped up dark chocolate and butter.
3. Mix well and pour over the cake.
4. Allow to set before cutting and serving the torte.

46

GLUTEN-FREE
CHOCOLATE CAKE

SERVES 8-10

ingredients

GLUTEN-FREE CHOCOLATE SPONGE:

180g Egg whites
190g Caster sugar
120g Egg yolks
52g Cocoa powder

CHOCOLATE MOUSSE:

200g Callebaut 823 NV, 33% milk
   chocolate
250g Whipping cream

**VANILLA MOUSSE AND
RASPBERRIES:**

60g Caster sugar
50g Egg yolks
250g Full-fat milk
½ Vanilla pod
4g (2 Leaves) gelatine, soaked
   in water
250g Whipping cream
1 Handful raspberries, fresh or frozen

TO FINISH:

Neutral glaze
Chocolate decorations

method

GLUTEN-FREE CHOCOLATE SPONGE:

1. Whisk the egg whites and sugar to form a
    stiff meringue.
2. Add lightly beaten egg yolks and then fold
    in the sieved cocoa powder.
3. Spread onto a lined baking tray and bake
    for 12 minutes at 190°C.

CHOCOLATE MOUSSE:

1. Melt the milk chocolate to 45°C and fold in
    the lightly whipped cream.
2. Line a 20x20cm frame with half the sponge
    and top with the chocolate mousse.
3. Place the other half of the sponge on top
    of the chocolate mousse.

VANILLA MOUSSE AND RASPBERRIES:

1. Whisk the sugar and egg yolks together.
2. Boil the milk and the vanilla pod together, then add the egg yolk/sugar mix and cook until 75°C.
3. Add the drained gelatine leaves.
4. Leave to cool then mix in the whipping cream.
5. Pour into the frame on top of the second sponge then add the raspberries (fresh or frozen are fine).
6. Place in a freezer until set.

TO FINISH:

1. Glaze with a neutral glaze.
2. Finish with chocolate decorations.

CHOCOLATE CHIP AND
BANANA LOAF

ENOUGH TO FILL A 1KG LOAF TIN

ingredients

125g Old bananas
125g Soft brown sugar
2 Large eggs
100g Plain flour
5g Baking powder
25g Cocoa powder
70g Butter
90g Dark chocolate drops
25g Flaked almonds
Cocoa powder, for dusting
Orange curd, to serve

method

1. Preheat the oven to 170°C.
2. Mash up the bananas in a small bowl and then place into a mixer with a whisk attachment, add the sugar and eggs then whisk until light and fluffy, like a thick meringue.
3. Sieve the flour, baking powder and cocoa powder together and, using a spatula, fold into the egg mix.
4. Melt the butter and 50g of chocolate drops together and fold them in as well.
5. Finally add the remaining 40g of chocolate drops.
6. Place the mix into a 1kg loaf tin lined with greaseproof paper, sprinkle with the almonds and cook in the middle of the oven for around 45-60 minutes or until a knife comes out clean from the centre of the cake.
7. When cooked, dust with cocoa powder and leave to cool.
8. Serve with orange curd.

51

CHOCOLATE CUP CAKES
DECORATED WITH A CHOCOLATE NEST AND MINI CHOCOLATE EGGS

MAKES 8 CUP CAKES

ingredients

SPONGE:

85g Self-raising flour
15g Cacao Barry Extra Brute
   Cocoa Powder
100g Butter
100g Caster sugar
100g Eggs

CHOCOLATE GLAZE:

150g Double cream
150g Callebaut 811NV dark chocolate

DECORATION:

150g Callebaut 811NV dark
   chocolate, melted
Mini chocolate eggs

method

SPONGE:

1. Sieve the flour and cocoa powder three times.
2. Cream the butter and sugar until light with a creamy texture.
3. Beat in the eggs a little at a time with a small amount of sieved powders.
4. Gently fold in the rest of the sieved powders.
5. Pipe into individual paper cases three-quarters full.
6. Bake at 180°C for approximately 15 minutes.

CHOCOLATE GLAZE:

1. While the cakes are cooking prepare the chocolate glaze by heating the cream and chocolate in a microwave for 1 minute on full power.
2. Stir well to create a smooth glaze.

ASSEMBLY:

1. Cool the cup cakes once cooked.
2. Cut the top off each cup cake at an angle.
3. Aerate half the chocolate glaze with a balloon whisk and pipe immediately on top of the cut cup cake with a star nozzle.
4. Replace the top of the cup cake.
5. Dip the cup cakes upside down in the remaining prepared glaze to give a shiny, even coating. If the glaze has set on cooling rewarm it in the microwave for 10 seconds to make a fluid glaze again.
6. For the nest decoration place melted Callebaut 811NV chocolate into a paper piping cone and pipe a fine lattice of lines on a frozen granite tile – about 20x10cm.
7. Lift the chocolate lattice off the tile immediately with a palette knife.
8. Concertina the lattice together and roll while still flexible to form a nest.
9. Place the chocolate nest immediately on each chocolate cup cake to stick to the setting glaze.
10. Finish the decoration with mini chocolate eggs.

CHOCOLATE AND COFFEE CAKE

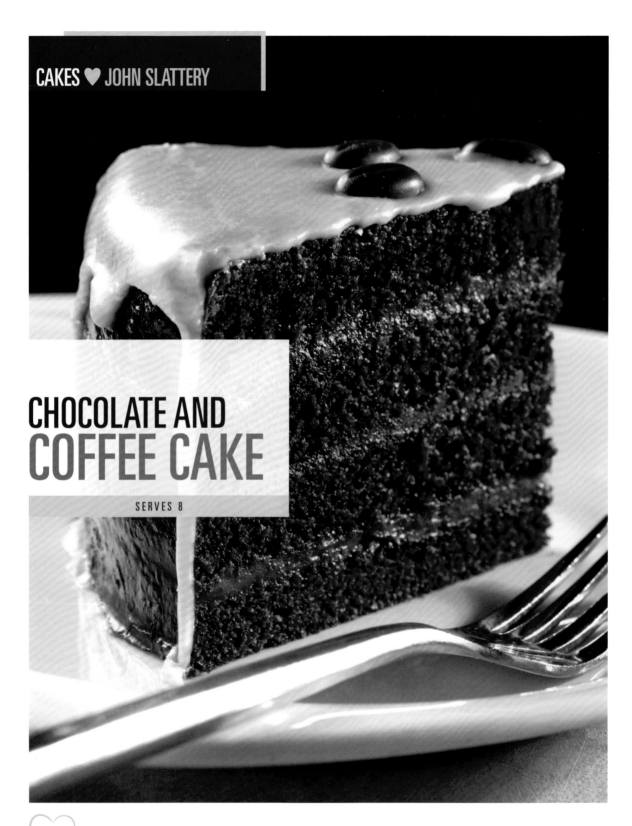

CHOCOLATE AND
COFFEE CAKE

SERVES 8

ingredients

CAKE:

100g Unsalted butter
200g Caster sugar
2 Whole eggs
45g Cocoa powder
5g Baking powder
5g Bicarbonate of soda
1 Pinch salt
170g Plain flour
160g Full-fat milk

COFFEE CUSTARD:

30g Golden syrup
250g Caster sugar
20g Instant coffee
300g Water
100g Cornflour
80g Water
45g Unsalted butter

ICING:

120g Icing sugar
20g Boiling water
A little instant coffee to flavour
    and colour

DECORATION:

A few chocolate coffee beans

method

CHOCOLATE AND COFFEE CAKE

1. In a mixer using a beater attachment, place the butter (at room temperature) along with the sugar. Cream together until light.
2. Add the eggs one at a time, beating well. Scrape down the bowl after each addition.
3. Sieve all the dry ingredients together, adding to the mixing bowl in two portions and mix on slow speed until the batter is clear.
4. Slowly stream in the milk.
5. Divide the mix between two greased and floured 18cm cake tins.
6. Bake at 170°C for 25-30 minutes.

CUSTARD:

1. Put the golden syrup, sugar, coffee and 300g water into a pan and bring to the boil, whisking occasionally.
2. Mix the cornflour with the 80g water, whisking briskly as you add this to the boiling mixture. The consistency should be that of thick glue (add a little more water if too thick).
3. Bring back to the boil, whisking all the time. Boil for a couple of minutes to ensure the cornflour is cooked.
4. Remove from the heat and add the butter.
5. Pour into a bowl, cover with cling film and chill in the refrigerator until cold and firm.

ASSEMBLY:

1. Skin the top crust off both cakes and split each into two discs.
2. Spread approximately 30 per cent of the custard onto each layer of cake as you pile them together.
3. Use the remaining custard to mask around the sides and top to seal the cake with a very thin layer of custard.
4. Mix the icing ingredients together and pour over the top of the cake, allowing it to flow down the sides here and there.
5. To complete, sprinkle with a few chocolate coffee beans.

SWISS FOREST GATEAU

SWISS FOREST GATEAU

SERVES 8

ingredients

CHOCOLATE SPONGE SHEET:

will make 2x18cm rounds
230g Egg yolks
150g Caster sugar
250g Egg whites
100g Caster sugar
60g Cornflour
60g Flour
50g Cocoa powder

CHOCOLATE CHANTILLY:

500g Whipping cream
50g Caster sugar
65g 70% dark chocolate, small pieces
    or callets
25g Cocoa masse CM-CAL

KIRSCH SYRUP:

100g Stock syrup (see p90)
25g Water
Kirsch, to taste (approximately 20g)

ASSEMBLY:

Morello cherries, in juice
Callebaut W2 NV melted white
    chocolate
Arrowroot or cornflour, as required
Whipping cream (optional)
Cocoa powder or icing sugar

method

CHOCOLATE SPONGE SHEET:

1. Whisk together the egg yolks and 150g sugar.
2. Whisk together the egg whites and 100g sugar.
3. Sieve together the cornflour, flour and cocoa powder.
4. Mix one-third of the stiff egg white into the yolk mix, then fold in the flour, cornflour and cocoa mix.
5. Fold in the remaining egg whites and spread mix on to a silpat/silicone paper 40x60cm.
6. Bake at 200°C for 8-10 minutes.

CHOCOLATE CHANTILLY:

1. Bring the cream and sugar to the boil in a pan.
2. Add the chocolate and cocoa masse and mix well.
3. Store in the refrigerator for 12-18 hours before use.

KIRSCH SYRUP:

1. Mix all ingredients together.

ASSEMBLY:

1. Cut the sponge into 18cm or 5cm diameter circles.
2. Place one sponge into a ring (18cm or 5cm diameter) and pipe the first layer of Chantilly over it.
3. Place a second sponge onto the cream and brush on some Kirsch syrup.
4. Pipe a second layer of Chantilly on it and sprinkle with some halved morello cherries.
5. Cover with a third sponge, brush with kirsch syrup and cover with a thin layer of Chantilly.
6. Chill or blast freeze and when firm remove the ring.
7. Thinly spread melted white chocolate on to a frozen piece of marble or steel tray.

8. Quickly cut off with a flat held knife and place a band of chocolate around the gateau and place some on top.
9. Heat some of the cherry juice and thicken with arrowroot or cornflour.
10. Mix with the rest of the cherries (whole) and cool, then place in the centre of the gateau in a 6-8cm circle (smaller circle for the individual cakes).
11. Decorate the edge with chocolate Chantilly or cream.
12. Dust with a little cocoa/icing sugar.

"THERE'S NOTHING BETTER THAN A GOOD FRIEND, EXCEPT A GOOD FRIEND WITH CHOCOLATE."

LINDA GRAYSON, "THE PICKWICK PAPERS"

63

GINGER AND CHOCOLATE CAKE

MAKES ENOUGH FOR A 1KG LOAF TIN OR 8-10 MINI CAKE LOAVES

ingredients

100g Callebaut 811 NV, 54% dark
   chocolate, chopped
3 tbsp Cocoa powder
250ml Ginger beer
250g Plain flour
1½ tsp Bicarbonate of soda
140g Caster sugar
1 tsp Ground ginger
3 tbsp Vegetable oil
40g Stem ginger, finely chopped

method

1. Preheat the oven to 170°C.
2. Line a 1kg loaf tin with greaseproof paper or if using mini tins butter then flour them.
3. Place the chocolate and cocoa powder in a large bowl.
4. Heat the beer in a saucepan until nearly boiling and then pour over the chocolate/cocoa powder. Leave to cool.
5. Sieve the flour, bicarbonate of soda, sugar, and ground ginger together and mix into the cool chocolate mix.
6. Add the oil and the stem ginger to the mix and when all incorporated spoon into the lined cake tin or mini loaf tins.
7. Bake for about 30-40 minutes or until cooked – springy to the touch. Small versions will take 10-15 minutes.

WHITE CHOCOLATE
CARROT CAKE

FILLS A 24CM SPRINGFORM MOULD TIN

ingredients

3 Large free-range eggs
200g Butter, melted
250g Caster sugar
5g Vanilla essence
150g Plain white flour
75g Wholemeal flour
6g Bicarbonate of soda
6g Baking powder
1 Pinch salt
4g Ground cinnamon
300g Grated carrots
100g Pecan nuts or walnuts, finely
  chopped
100g White chocolate chunks

TO FINISH:

100ml Single cream
120g Callebaut W2 NV white
  chocolate
Pecans or walnuts, to decorate
  (dependent on those used in the
  cake)
Strawberry or raspberry sauce,
  to serve
Whipped cream, to serve

method

1. In a large bowl combine the eggs, butter, caster sugar and the vanilla essence. In a separate bowl sift together the white and brown flours with the bicarbonate of soda, baking powder, salt and cinnamon.
2. Fold the egg, butter, sugar and vanilla mixture into the dry ingredients, then add the grated carrots, chopped pecans or walnuts. Finally add the white chocolate chunks.
3. Pour the dough into a greased springform mould and bake at 175°C for 40-50 minutes. Check with a skewer – if the cake is thoroughly cooked it should come out clean. Allow the cake to cool before taking it out of the mould.

TO FINISH:

1. Heat the cream in the microwave and add the white chocolate. Whisk until smooth.
2. Spread this glaze over the top of the carrot cake and decorate with either pecans or walnuts.
3. Serve a slice with a strawberry or raspberry sauce and some whipped cream.

ROYALE

SERVES 8-10

ingredients

SPONGE:

562g Egg whites
125g Caster sugar
337g Icing sugar
180g Ground almonds
187g Hazelnut powder
187g Full-fat milk
100g Plain flour

PRALINE BASE:

125g Callebaut W2 NV
    white chocolate
500g Praline paste
200g Feuilletine

CHOCOLATE MOUSSE:

250g milk chocolate, small pieces
    or callets
500g Whipping cream

TO FINISH:

Chocolate for spraying or
    icing sugar and cocoa
    powder
Chocolate decorations

method

SPONGE:

1. Whisk the egg whites and caster sugar to form a stiff meringue.
2. Sieve the icing sugar, ground almonds and the hazelnut powder, mix with the milk then fold into the meringue and add the flour.
3. Spread onto baking paper on a tray and bake at 190°C for 15 minutes.

PRALINE LAYER:

1. Melt the white chocolate, mix with the praline paste and add the feuilletine.
2. Line a 20x20cm frame with the sponge. Spread the praline on top of the sponge.

CHOCOLATE MOUSSE:

1. Melt the milk chocolate to 45°C and fold in the lightly whipped cream.
2. Pour into the frame on top of the sponge and praline.
3. Put in the freezer until set.

TO FINISH:

1. Remove the frame when set and spray with a chocolate spray gun. Alternatively, dust with a mixture of icing sugar and cocoa powder.
2. Add some chocolate decorations to finish.

RICH CHOCOLATE
FRUIT CAKE

MAKES A 20CM ROUND CAKE

ingredients

350g Currants
150g Sultanas
150g Raisins
70g Dried cherries
100ml Chocolate liquor (alcohol)
1 Orange, zest and juice
175g Unsalted butter
175g Soft dark brown sugar
3 Large eggs
2 tbsp Molasses
175g Plain flour
40g Cocoa powder
1 tsp Ground cinnamon
1 tsp Ground ginger
100g Chocolate drops
50g Ground hazelnuts
Chocolate marzipan, to decorate
Chocolate sugar paste, to decorate

method

1. Soak the fruit in the chocolate liquor, orange zest and juice and leave for 24 hours to marinate.
2. Preheat the oven to 150°C. Line a 20cm round cake tin with a double lining of greaseproof paper.
3. Cream the butter and sugar together until light and fluffy, then start adding the eggs one at a time until all combined.
4. Add the molasses.
5. Sieve the flour, cocoa powder, cinnamon and ginger together and fold into the mix as well.
6. Finally add the chocolate drops and hazelnuts.
7. Spoon the mix into the cake tin and cook for 2-2½ hours or until cooked (if the top of the cake becomes too dark during cooking place a piece of greaseproof paper on top).
8. When the cake has cooled coat with chocolate marzipan and chocolate sugar paste. and decorate for any occasion.

DRUNKEN CHOCOLATE CAKE

SERVES 12

ingredients

500g Chocolate cake, broken into
 small pieces
300g Brandy
500g Digestive biscuits, broken
400g Fresh whipping cream
1.2kg Dark chocolate

DECORATION:

200g Digestive biscuit crumbs, sieved
 to remove fine particles

method

1. Prepare a 25cm cake hoop by sitting it on to a plastic sheet on a metal tray. Line around the inside of the hoop with a strip of acetate.
2. Place the chocolate cake pieces into a bowl, add the brandy and allow to absorb. Stir occasionally to ensure all the cake is moist.
3. Add the broken digestive biscuits and mix in.
4. Bring the cream to the boil and pour onto the chocolate. Stir to allow the heat from the cream to melt the chocolate.
5. When a smooth ganache is achieved, add this to the other ingredients and mix thoroughly.
6. Pour the mix into the prepared cake hoop.
7. Place into the refrigerator overnight.
8. Remove from the refrigerator, remove the metal hoop and peel away the acetate strip.

DECORATION:

1. Using a heat gun (or a hair dryer) warm the surface of the cake.
2. Press the biscuit crumbs around the sides and over the top.
3. Mark with the back of a knife blade into portions.

NOTE:

The brandy can be substituted with most other spirits or liqueurs; Amaretto, Grand Marnier, Baileys Irish Cream or a mellow whisky all work well.

The flavour of this cake improves with allowing to mature for a day or two in an airtight container in a cool place, before final decoration and serving.

ALMOND, POLENTA
AND CHOCOLATE CAKES

MAKES 24 INDIVIDUAL CAKES

ingredients

500g Salted butter
200g Caster sugar
5 Large free-range eggs
50ml Orange juice, freshly squeezed
  and zests retained
50ml Buttermilk
600g Ground almonds
200g Polenta
450g Mixed fruit: sultanas, chopped
  apricots, goji berries, cranberries,
  candied peel, including the orange
  zests from above
15g Baking powder
200g Small bake-stable dark
  chocolate chips
Icing sugar, to serve

method

1. Whisk the butter and caster sugar together in a mixing bowl on a low speed, then add the eggs one by one followed by the orange juice and buttermilk.
2. Mix all the remaining dry ingredients together and pour on a slow speed into the wet ingredients. Beat lightly for 1 minute.
3. Spoon into round silicone cake moulds 8x4cm deep.
4. Bake at 165°C for 30 minutes.
5. Allow to cool in the silicone moulds then take out the cakes, place on a serving plate and dust with icing sugar. Store in an air-tight container or freeze.

NOTE:

This recipe can be easily adapted as a gluten-free cake by simply replacing the baking powder with a gluten-free baking powder. Bake-stable chocolate chips resist oven temperatures of up to 200°C and are ideal to add to bread, croissants, brioches, cakes or pastry bases. Bake-stable chocolate comes in a wide variety of shapes and sizes from sticks to small drops and large chunks in milk, white and dark chocolate.

CHOCOLATE
WHOOPIE PIES

MAKES 12-15 PIES

ingredients

115g Butter
200g Caster sugar
1 Large egg
225ml Skimmed milk
280g Plain flour
50g Cocoa powder
2½ tsp Bicarbonate of soda

FILLING:

50ml Skimmed milk
100g White marshmallows
½ Vanilla pod
115g Unsalted butter
100g Icing sugar

ICING:

50g Icing sugar
25g Cocoa powder
4 tbsp Water

method

1. Preheat the oven to 170°C.
2. Cream the butter and sugar together until light and fluffy, then add the egg.
3. Add the milk slowly to the mix and keep mixing until it is all incorporated.
4. Sieve the flour with the cocoa powder and bicarbonate of soda, then fold into the mix as well.
5. Line a baking tray with parchment paper and, using a piping bag filled with the mix, pipe 4cm disc shapes.
6. Bake in the oven for 10-15 minutes or until cooked.

FILLING:

1. Heat the milk in a saucepan and place in the marshmallows, stir around until they have melted. Remove from the heat and stir in the vanilla pod seeds.
2. Cream the butter and sugar together in a mixer with a paddle and when the marshmallow mix has cooled add it in. Mix until you reach a light and fluffy consistency. When cooled spoon or pipe onto one whoopie pie and place another on top to make a whoopie sandwich.

ICING:

1. Mix the sugar and cocoa powder with the water until it becomes a runny fondant icing – you may need more water. Spoon on top of the whoopie pies and then decorate as desired.

ORIGINE

SERVES 8-10

ingredients

SPONGE:

300g Almond powder
260g Egg yolks
75g Butter
60g Cocoa powder
280g Egg whites
100g Caster sugar
125g Plain flour

CHOCOLATE MOUSSE:

450g Stock syrup
225g Egg yolks
370g Tanzania 70% dark chocolate,
    small pieces or callets
750g Whipping cream
450g Papouasie or 35% milk
    chocolate, small pieces or callets
750g Whipping cream

GLAZE:

250g Full-fat milk
200g Callebaut 811 NV, 54% dark
    chocolate
150g Stock syrup
200g Bakers chocolate
    (pate a glacer)

TO FINISH:

Chocolate shapes and curls

method

SPONGE:

1. Mix the almond powder, egg yolks, butter and cocoa powder together until they form a paste.
2. Whisk the egg whites and sugar into a meringue then fold into the paste and fold in the flour.
3. Bake in a 20cm round tin at 190°C for 20 minutes.

CHOCOLATE MOUSSE:

1. Boil the syrup and pour over the egg yolks.
2. Cook over a bain-marie until the temperature is 65°C.
3. Remove from the heat and whisk until the mixture is stiff and cool.
4. Split the mixture into two bowls.
5. Melt the Tanzania dark chocolate in the microwave until 47°C.
6. Lightly whip 750g cream.
7. Add one half of the mix and half of the whipped cream to the melted Tanzania chocolate, mixing quickly, then fold in the rest of the cream.
8. Cut the sponge in half and place in the bottom of a 20cm ring.
9. Pour the dark chocolate mousse over the sponge then top with the other half of the sponge.
10. Melt the milk chocolate in the microwave until 47°C and make the milk chocolate mousse using the same method as the dark chocolate mousse.
11. Add as a top layer, smooth with palette knife.

GLAZE:

1. Bring the milk to the boil and pour over the finely chopped chocolate.
2. Add the syrup and finally the melted bakers chocolate. Make sure it is mixed well then glaze the cake over a wire rack.
3. Pour the glaze over the top and let it run over the sides.

TO FINISH:

1. Decorate with chocolate shapes and curls.

CONFECTIONERY

TRUFFLE MEN

MAKES 15-20

ingredients

RASPBERRY GANACHE:

makes 30-40 shells:

100g Raspberry purée
60g Whipping cream
20g Glucose
175g Callebaut 811 NV, 54% dark
  chocolate
15-20g Brandy
4-5g Raspberry eau de vie (optional)

COFFEE GANACHE:

30-40 Shells
100g Whipping cream
20g Glucose
6g Instant coffee
210g Callebaut W2 NV
  white chocolate

ASSEMBLY:

Truffle shells: 40 dark, 20 white, 20 milk
Melted chocolate
Tempered chocolate
Chocolate discs
Marzipan
Royal icing
210g Callebaut W2 NV
  white chocolate

method

RASPBERRY GANACHE:

This recipe fills around 40 shells.
1. Bring the purée, cream and glucose to the boil.
2. Pour onto the chocolate.
3. At 30°C add the brandy and eau de vie, if using.

COFFEE GANACHE:

This recipe fills around 40 shells.
1. Bring the cream and glucose to the boil in a pan.
2. Add the coffee.
3. Pour onto the chocolate and mix well.
4. Use at 27°C for filling.

ASSEMBLY:

1. Fill the white and milk shells with coffee ganache and the dark shells with raspberry ganache.
2. Seal with melted chocolate and stick two together.
3. Place onto a chocolate disc and allow to set.
4. Pipe out small dots of tempered chocolate 1-2cm diameter as a 'beret'.
5. Decorate the top shell as a face using marzipan or royal icing and place the beret on top.

WHITE CHOCOLATE FUDGE

MAKES 100 SQUARES

ingredients

600g Caster sugar
225g Liquid glucose
225g Unsalted butter, diced
550g Whipping cream
50g Vanilla paste
500g Callebaut W2 NV
    white chocolate

DECORATION:

150g Callebaut W2 NV
    white chocolate, tempered
15g Callebaut 823 NV, 33% milk
    chocolate, tempered and in a
    piping bag

method

1. Slowly bring all the ingredients, except the chocolate, up to the boil – 120ºC (hard ball stage).
2. Lift off the heat and mix in the chocolate.
3. Pour onto a cling film lined tray 12x38cm.
4. Allow to set.
5. When completely cold and firm coat the top with a thin layer of white chocolate.
6. Remove from the tray and discard the cling film.
7. Coat the other side with a thin layer of white chocolate and decorate with a swirl of milk chocolate to form the top of the product.
8. Cut into small squares.

NOTE:

This fudge will keep for a month if you keep it airtight or if you can keep your hands off it that long!

The basic recipe may be used, substituting milk or dark chocolate to create contrasting varieties.

MILK CHOCOLATE MINT BARS AND
DARK CHOCOLATE CHILLI BARS

MAKES 5 X 100G BARS

ingredients

MILK CHOCOLATE FLAVOURED WITH FRESH MINT:

10g Fresh mint leaves
25g Cocoa butter, melted
500g Callebaut 823 NV, 33% chocolate

DARK CHOCOLATE FLAVOURED WITH CRUSHED POWDERED CHILLIES:

5g Crushed powdered chillies
25g Cocoa butter, melted
500g Callebaut 811 NV, 54% dark chocolate

method

1. Chop or grind the plants or spices as finely as possible to release their aroma and flavour.
2. Place into the melted cocoa butter and mix thoroughly.
3. Leave to rest overnight.
4. The next day melt the cocoa butter to 50°C and strain.
5. Cool to 30°C and blend into pre-crystallised chocolate.
6. Mould. Allow to set and enjoy the natural flavours!

Recipes as featured in Jean Pierre Wybauw's book
Fine Chocolates 2 – Great Ganache Experience.

86

COCOA NIB GIANDUJA

MAKES 50 PIECES

ingredients

100g 45%+ Almond marzipan
75g Fine hazelnut praline
100g 33% Madagascar Tanariva
   milk chocolate
30g Cocoa nibs
100g Plantation Alto El Sol Peru 65%
   dark chocolate

method

1. Roll the marzipan into a 2mm thick 15cm square and place in a flexi-silicone baking tray of at least 15mm depth.
2. Slightly warm the praline and mix thoroughly with the melted tempered milk chocolate and nibs.
3. Pour onto the marzipan and wait until the wet shine completely disappears and it has just set.
4. Pour over the dark chocolate. For decoration, if desired, it is possible to do some rapid piping and feathering with a fork, but this must be done quickly before the dark chocolate has set.
5. As soon as the chocolate is dry to the touch, mark and cut into pieces with a long knife.

SARAH BERNHARDT

MAKES 25

ingredients

**RASPBERRY SEMI-CONFIT
(OR RASPBERRIES IN SYRUP):**

100g Syrup (see below)
100g Frozen raspberries
50g Brandy
10g Raspberry eau de vie (optional)

STOCK SYRUP:

700g Granulated sugar
100g Glucose
500g Water

LIGHT BUTTER GANACHE:

250g Soft butter
150g Fondant or icing sugar
250g Callebaut 811 NV, 54% dark
    chocolate (tempered) or 375g
    Callebaut 823 NV, 33% milk
    chocolate (tempered)

ASSEMBLY:

Soft macaroons, flavour of
your choice

method

RASPBERRY SEMI-CONFIT (OR RASPBERRIES IN SYRUP):

1. Boil the syrup.
2. Pour over the frozen raspberries in a bowl.
3. Add the brandy and the eau de vie, if using.
4. Cover with cling film and refrigerate for 24 hours.

STOCK SYRUP:

1. Mix all the ingredients and boil for 1 minute exactly.

LIGHT BUTTER GANACHE:

1. Cream together the butter and fondant/icing sugar.
2. In a steady stream, pour in the tempered chocolate and whisk to an airy but stable consistency.

ASSEMBLY:

1. Spread a little butter ganache on the macaroons then place a well drained raspberry on top.
2. Pipe butter ganache in a peak shape over it, using a plain piping tube.
3. Let until well set, then enrobe in dark or milk couverture. Decorate to your choice.

CHOCOLATE LACE BOWLS AND SPHERES

MAKES 4

ingredients

1 kg 70% Dark chocolate

Equipment

Polycarbonate mould, semi-sphere
  approx 12cm diameter
Small piping bags
Palette knife

method

1. Place the mould in a freezer for 1 hour.
2. Melt the chocolate in a microwave. Retain the temper by stirring frequently until the chocolate begins to melt. Stop heating when about 5-10% of the chocolate is still solid, which should then be dissolved by stirring it into the rest of the chocolate. Thicker, more heavily tempered chocolate is ideal.
3. Fill the piping bag and remove the mould from the freezer.
4. Wipe any condensation from the inner surface of the mould to prevent sticking and start piping immediately by 'dropping' small, interconnected loops of chocolate. Start from the centre and work outwards right up to the rim. Finish the rim with a solid line of chocolate and scrape the flat surface clean with the palette knife.
5. After refrigerating for 20 minutes or until the chocolate has detached from the mould, remove the semi-sphere carefully, using a fingernail to detach the chocolate around the rim. Pushing on one side should then swivel it out of the mould.
6. Either upturn and use as a serving bowl for dessert items or enclose them in a sphere for decoration. To do this place two semi-spheres on a warm plate until the full circle of the rim begins to melt, then simply drop one semi-sphere precisely on top of the other.
7. After 5 minutes or when set, food colouring can then be applied with a soft paintbrush or clean buffing cloth.

CHOCOLATE LATTICEWORK BUTTERFLIES

SERVES 4

ingredients

1kg 64% Madagascar Manjari
   dark chocolate

Equipment

Silicone sugarcraft butterfly mould
Small piping bags
Palette knife
Silicone paper

method

1. Melt the chocolate in a microwave. Retain the temper by stirring frequently until the chocolate begins to melt. Stop heating when about 5-10% of the chocolate is still solid, which should then be dissolved by stirring it into the rest of the chocolate.

2. Pour a generous amount of chocolate over the surface of the mould and scrape with the palette knife until the top surface shows through.

3. Refrigerate for 20 minutes or until set.

4. Carefully remove from the mould by placing upside down and peeling the mould back from the chocolate form.

5. Fill the piping bag and pipe a latticework on the underside of the butterfly which radiates outwards – thicker and denser at the inside edge of the wings.

6. Once set, place two wings together in an appropriate flying position, with the outer edges raised on upturned bowls or cups and the inner edges resting on a small strip of silicone paper.

7. Pipe the body of the butterfly to join the wings securely.

8. After 20 minutes or when set, food colouring can then be applied with a soft paintbrush or clean buffing cloth.

MILK YORKSHIRE CHOCOLATE

144 BONBONS PER FRAME

ingredients

MILK GANACHE:

200g Yorkshire cream
500g Callebaut 823 NV, 33% milk
  chocolate
40g Yorkshire butter
10g Rapeseed oil from Collingham,
  Wetherby
Callebaut 823 NV, 33% milk
  chocolate, tempered for coating

method

MILK GANACHE:

1. Bring the cream to the boil and pour over the chocolate, butter and rapeseed oil.
2. Mix well until combined and leave to set in a frame for 24 hours.
3. When set, coat the bottom of the ganache with tempered milk chocolate.
4. Cut into small squares the size required and dip each one into tempered milk chocolate. Place onto a cocoa butter transfer or textured plastic sheet and leave to set.

"ALL I REALLY NEED IS LOVE, BUT A LITTLE CHOCOLATE NOW AND THEN DOESN'T HURT!"

LUCY VAN PELT (IN PEANUTS, BY CHARLES M. SCHULZ)

NERO DELIGHT

MAKES 40

ingredients

250g Soft butter
150g Icing sugar
100g Whole eggs
300g Plain flour
1 Pinch cinnamon
50g Cocoa masse CM-CAL, melted
Apricot jam, boiled
Callebaut 811 NV, 54% dark
   chocolate, to cover

method

1. Preheat the oven to 220°C.
2. Cream the butter and sugar well, then add the eggs.
3. Fold in the flour, cinnamon and melted cocoa masse.
4. Mix well.
5. Pipe the mixture into rosettes (with a star tube) onto silpats and bake for 5-7 minutes.
6. Place aside to cool, then cover the flat side with boiled apricot jam and allow to dry.
7. Cover with dark cocoa masse and place onto transfer sheets or mark as you wish.

NOTE:

If you wish you can sprinkle cocoa nibs onto the piped rosettes before baking.

MANCHESTER TART
CHOCOLATES

MAKES 36 CHOCOLATES

ingredients

250g Callebaut 823 NV, 33% milk
   chocolate required (up to 1kg to
   work with)
75g Raspberry jam
   (of good quality)
75g Desiccated coconut

**'CUSTARD' FILLING – WHITE
CHOCOLATE GANACHE:**

135g Whipping cream
35g Liquid glucose
3 Drops vanilla compound*
10g Custard powder
270g Callebaut W2 NV
   white chocolate, broken into
   pieces
* Vanilla compound – use a good
   quality concentrated vanilla.

NOTE:

These chocolates are best enjoyed
eaten fresh, because the ganache
filling is exposed (not sealed in with
chocolate to protect it) and the air
will dry it out. Store in a dark airtight
container and eat within 3 weeks.

method

1. Mould a chocolate case in milk chocolate (I have used 'chocolate world' mould number 1241) Allow to set.
2. Although each empty chocolate case weighs only 7g remember you will need to temper additional chocolate to allow for filling the moulds, emptying and working with the chocolate – the excess can be used again.
3. Pipe a generous bulb (2g) of raspberry jam into the base of each set chocolate case.

'CUSTARD' FILLING – WHITE CHOCOLATE GANACHE:

1. Bring to the boil the cream and the glucose with the vanilla, then whisk in the custard powder.
2. Pour onto the chocolate, leave for 1 minute and then stir to combine the ingredients.
3. Stir occasionally until all the chocolate is melted
4. Leave to cool completely (better to cover with plastic to prevent skinning). I find it better to make this the day before and allow to stand overnight at room temperature.
5. Put the ganache into the machine bowl of an electric mixer fitted with a beater, then aerate on medium speed for approximately 4 minutes.
6. Put the ganache in a Savoy piping bag fitted with a 7/8cm plain tube (nozzle).
7. Pipe the ganache to seal over the jam in the base and fill just over the brim of the chocolate case.
8. Sprinkle with desiccated coconut.
9. Allow to set.

SNOBINETTE CHICKS

MAKES 25

ingredients

LIMONCELLO BUTTER CREAM:

200g Soft butter
200g Fondant or icing sugar
30-50g Hot water
Vanilla essence, to taste
Limoncello, to taste

ASSEMBLY:

Dark or milk snobinettes
  chocolate cups
Plain sponge discs (see praline
  chocolate tart p188)
Passion fruit syrup
Passion fruit topping
Yellow sugar
Royal icing

method

LIMONCELLO BUTTER CREAM:

1. Cream the butter well.
2. Add the fondant in pieces or the icing sugar if using and blend together.
3. Add the hot water.
4. Finish with vanilla essence and Limoncello as desired.

ASSEMBLY:

1. Place a small round of vanilla sponge on bottom of each snobinette chocolate cup.
2. Brush with passion fruit syrup and pipe some passion fruit topping on top.
3. Pipe butter cream over it in a dome shape.
4. Pipe a small blob of butter cream on top (as the head) and sprinkle with dry yellow sugar.
5. Decorate the head of chick using royal icing.

CHOCOLATE DIPPED
CANDIED FRUIT

SERVES 10

ingredients

1kg Caster sugar
1kg Honey
1500ml Water
1kg Whole fruit eg. cherries,
    clementines or sliced fruit eg.
    pineapple, oranges
300g 75% Tanzanie dark chocolate,
    melted

method

1. Boil the sugar, honey and water in a heavy saucepan, stirring constantly, until it reaches 112°C.
2. Add the small fruit whole or large fruit sliced and simmer until the fruit is translucent.
3. Drain and cool then leave to dry overnight.
4. Use skewers or toothpicks to dip the fruit in the melted chocolate.
5. Fill a piping bag with melted chocolate and decorate as desired. Leave to set for at least 1 hour or until the chocolate has fully contracted and squeezed any excess juice from the fruit.

QUICK CONFIT
GRAPEFRUIT SKINS

MAKES 25

ingredients

STOCK SYRUP:

400g Granulated sugar
75g Glucose
750g Water

CONFIT GRAPEFRUIT SKINS:

1 Grapefruit
Stock syrup (see above)
Caster sugar, as required
Callebaut 811 NV, 54% dark
  chocolate

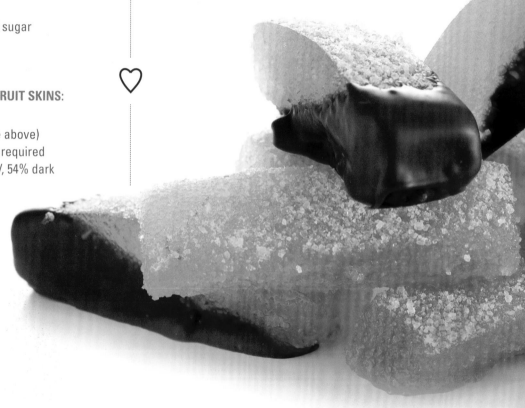

method

STOCK SYRUP:

1. Boil all the ingredients together for 1 minute exactly.

CONFIT GRAPEFRUIT SKINS:

1. Cut the grapefruit skins off squarely with some flesh attached, then cut into rectangular pieces approximately 2x4.5cm.
2. Bring the cut pieces to the boil in fresh water, strain and repeat three times.
3. Place drained pieces into the syrup, covered with a cartouche and simmer for approximately 2 hours.
4. Strain, cool and roll in the sugar.
5. Dip one end in the chocolate.

CHOCOLATE TRUFFLE

MAKES 15-20 TRUFFLES

ingredients

200ml Whipping cream
200g Callebaut 70-30-38 NV
   70% cocoa solids dark chocolate
75g Butter
150g Chocolate, for rolling
150g Cocoa powder, for rolling

method

1. Heat the cream in a saucepan until it reaches boiling point.
2. Remove from the heat and allow the cream to cool slightly.
3. Pour onto the chocolate and stir it very slowly until all the chocolate has melted.
4. Cut the butter into very small cubes, add to the chocolate mix and stir until melted (if you find the butter is not melting place it in a microwave for 10 seconds and stir again).
5. Place in a container in the refrigerator and leave overnight until set.
6. Roll into small balls about 2.5cm across, place on a tray and return to the fridge.
7. Wear plastic gloves to roll the chocolates with your hands in a little chocolate to coat the outside of the truffle, and then roll in cocoa powder.

CHOCOLATE DISCS WITH
FRUIT AND SEEDS

MAKES APPROX 20 DISCS

ingredients

250g Callebaut 811 NV, 54% dark chocolate

Multi-seeds – pumpkin, sunflower, flax

Fruit – raisins, goji berries, cranberries

method

1. Melt the chocolate carefully in the microwave – heat at full power for 30 seconds, stir, heat for 10 seconds, stir and continue melting for 10 seconds at a time and then stir until the whole mass has melted to 32°C – do not heat above 34°C otherwise the chocolate will not set as you will have destroyed the manufactured crystal form of the cocoa butter.
2. Pipe the chocolate into discs about 3cm in diameter onto silicone paper.
3. Lift the paper and shake to flatten the piped discs.
4. Sprinkle immediately with the multi-seeds and fruit.
5. Allow to set and serve when required.

P.C.P.
— PINE NUT, CRANBERRY AND PRALINE

MAKES 20 SLICES

This recipe can also be formed into a sheet. Cut into small squares and then fully enrobe in chocolate.

ingredients

400g Praline paste
200g Callebaut 823 NV, 33%
   milk chocolate, tempered
100g Feuilletine
35g Toasted pine nuts
25g Dried cranberries
100g Callebaut 823 NV, 33%
   milk chocolate, tempered,
   for decoration

method

1. Combine all the ingredients except the chocolate together.
2. Leave to firm slightly.
3. Deposit onto two 38cm squares of cling film.
4. Roll up to form 'sausages' 20-23cm in length.
5. Refrigerate for at least 2 hours to allow to firm up.
6. Unroll, remove and discard the cling film.
7. Coat with milk chocolate using a knife or brush to form a 'tree bark' effect.
8. Present in cut slices – delicious!

NOTE:

To create a contrast use dark chocolate to coat the roll with, white chocolate can look particularly festive. And of course the inclusions can be swapped about to form different initials …

W.P.C. Walnut, Praline Cashew
R.B.P. Raisin, Brazil, Praline
G.P.H. Ginger, Praline, Hazel

The possibilities are limited only by your imagination and good taste.

MARRON FANTASIE (CHESTNUTS)

MAKES 30

ingredients

MARRON FILLING:

315g Praline nut paste
115g Callebaut 823 NV, 33% milk chocolate, melted
110g Callebaut 811 NV, 54% dark chocolate, melted
65g Butter

ASSEMBLY:

Truffle shells or half spheres x 2
Melted chocolate
Green marzipan
Stock syrup
White and green royal icing
Red or brown food colouring (optional).

method

MARRON FILLING:

1. Mix all the ingredients together well.

ASSEMBLY:

2. Fill the truffle shells/spheres with the marron filling and allow to set.
3. Cover the opening with melted chocolate.
4. Roll out the marzipan to 4mm thick and cut out circles 25mm in diameter.
5. Place two together (overlapping) and brush with syrup.
6. Part enclose the shells in it.
7. Pipe small dots (triangular peaks) of green royal icing on to the marzipan – they can then be sprayed with the food colouring, if using.
8. Cover the join of marzipan and shell with a line of white royal icing. Place on a 2-3cm circle of chocolate for presentation.

DESSERTS

BAILEYS WHITE CHOCOLATE MOUSSE

SERVES 6 - 8

ingredients

300ml Full-fat milk
45g Custard powder
30g Vanilla sugar
250g Callebaut W2 NV
   white chocolate callets
30g Mycryo® cocoa butter
50ml Baileys Irish cream liqueur
400g Whipped cream (soft peaks)

method

1. Mix the milk, custard powder and vanilla sugar together and cook in a microwave oven, stirring regularly until cooked and of a very thick consistency.
2. While the custard is still hot add the white chocolate callets bit by bit and stir until totally dissolved. Next add the Mycryo® cocoa butter and the Baileys Irish Cream liqueur. Cool to about 30°C then fold in the whipped cream.
3. Cut a 5cm wide clear acetate or grease proof paper into 24cm strips and line 8x8cm diameter steel rings and place on a tray. Using a piping bag fitted with a large nozzle, pipe the mousse into the lined steel rings. Take a pallet knife and smooth the mousse level with the top of the acetate or grease proof paper.
4. Place the filled rings in the deep freeze for 6-8 hours. Take out of the freezer and remove the steel rings before carefully peeling off the acetate or grease proof paper. Place the mousse on a dessert plate. Allow to thaw in the fridge for 4 hours before serving.

TO SERVE:

1. Pipe in glasses or use as a component to layer a cake or as the main filling in a Yule chocolate log.

NOTE:

1. Decorate with a chocolate cigarillo, some berries and a few stripes of dark chocolate.
2. Alternatively pipe the mousse into glasses and decorate as shown or use the mousse to layer a cake or as the main component for a Baileys Yule Log.

CHESTNUT CHOCOLATE TORTE

SERVES 16

ingredients

350g Chestnut purée
140ml Full-fat milk
80g Caster sugar
90g Brown sugar
255g Unsalted butter
240g 75% Peru Piura Porcelana dark chocolate
4 Egg whites

method

1. Preheat the oven to 180°C.
2. Grease and line a 23cm round tin.
3. Heat the chestnut purée and milk then whisk in the sugars.
4. Melt the butter and chocolate in a bowl over steaming water.
5. Combine the chocolate and purée mix.
6. Whisk the egg whites to form stiff peaks, then fold into the chocolate mixture.
7. Pour the mix into the prepared tin and bake for 30 minutes, removing from the oven when set (there should only be slight movement in the middle).
8. Allow to cool before serving.

SMOOTH CHOCOLATE PANCAKES SERVED WITH CHOCOLATE ICE CREAM AND WARM CHERRIES TOPPED WITH CHOCOLATE SAUCE

SERVES 4

ingredients

SMOOTH CHOCOLATE PANCAKES:

2 Eggs
50g Caster sugar
600ml Semi-skimmed milk
220g Plain flour
20g Cacao Barry Extra Brute
    Cocoa Powder
30g Butter, melted
Oil, for frying

CHOCOLATE SAUCE:

150g Double cream
150g Callebaut 811 NV, 54% dark
    chocolate

TO SERVE:

Small tub chocolate ice cream
150g Fresh cherries warmed in light
    sugar syrup flavoured with a
    splash of Kirsch

method

SMOOTH CHOCOLATE PANCAKES:

1. Whisk together the eggs and sugar until the sugar is dissolved.
2. Whisk in the milk.
3. Pour in stages onto sieved flour and cocoa powder, whisking each portion to create a smooth batter.
4. Stir in the melted butter.
5. Place a small amount of oil into a frying pan.
6. Pour in sufficient batter to just cover the base of the pan, allow to set and cook on the bottom side.
7. Turn over with a palette knife and continue cooking this side to the same colour.
8. Turn over onto a square of silicone paper – pile up the pancakes as you continue cooking them.

CHOCOLATE SAUCE:

1. Melt the cream and chocolate together for 1 minute in a microwave at full power just before serving.

TO SERVE:

1. Once cool, fill each pancake with two small scoops of chocolate ice cream. Wrap to create a parcel.
2. Spoon over the Kirsch cherries.
3. Spoon over hot chocolate sauce and serve immediately.

125

MILK CHOCOLATE SWIRL FILLED WITH JAVA ORIGIN CHOCOLATE MOUSSE

SERVES 4

ingredients

CHOCOLATE SWIRL CYLINDERS:

250-300g Callebaut 823 NV, 33% milk
   chocolate

JAVA ORIGIN CHOCOLATE MOUSSE:

200ml Full-fat milk
35g Custard powder
20g Caster sugar
20g Mycryo® cocoa butter
250g Callebaut origins Java
   milk chocolate
400ml Whipped cream (soft peaks)

TO SERVE:

4 Chocolate swirl cylinders
   (see recipe opposite)
Some chocolate sponge
10ml Kirsch
300g Callebaut origins Java
   chocolate mousse
Some red berries, physalis and a
   Callebaut W2 NV white chocolate
   trellis to decorate

method

MILK CHOCOLATE SWIRL:

1. Pour the milk chocolate onto a frozen marble slab and smooth it out in an oblong piece 24x35cm.
2. Cut this piece into four equal strips and gently roll into cylinders of about 6cm in diameter, allowing a piece of 4cm to stick out. Leave the cylinders to crystallise.

JAVA ORIGIN CHOCOLATE MOUSSE:

1. Mix the milk, custard powder and caster sugar together and with a microwave make a thick custard, stirring regularly.
2. When the custard is cooked add the Mycryo® cocoa butter and bit by bit the Java Origin milk chocolate.
3. When cool (25°C) fold in the whipped cream. The mousse is now ready to be piped.

TO SERVE:

1. Place a chocolate swirl on a plate. Cut out of the sponge round discs the diameter of the cylinder and soak them with some kirsch.
2. Place one disc on the bottom of the cylinder and fill the cylinder half-way with the mousse. Place another disc in the middle and finish with a nice swirl of the mousse to the top of the cylinder.
3. Decorate with berries and physalis and stick a white chocolate trellis on top.

126

CHOCOLATE AND
TOFFOC SOUFFLE

MAKES 10

ingredients

PASTRY CREAM:

80g 70-30-38, 70% dark chocolate,
   small pieces or callets
4 Egg yolks
50g Caster sugar
30g Plain flour
250g Full-fat milk
1 Vanilla pod

MERINGUE:

8 Egg whites
150g Caster sugar
40g Toffoc Vodka
   (delicious toffee vodka)

method

PASTRY CREAM:

1. Mix the egg yolks, sugar and flour together.
2. Boil the milk and vanilla.
3. Pour onto the yolk mixture and whisk well together.
4. Return to the pan until the sauce thickens, whisking all the time.
5. Pour into a clean bowl and place cling film over the surface to prevent a skin forming.
6. Allow the pastry cream to cool a little then mix in the liqueur.

MERINGUE:

1. Whisk the egg whites until fluffy.
2. Add the sugar to produce a firm meringue.
3. Add a little of the meringue into the pastry cream and mix until smooth.
4. Fold in the remaining meringue and chocolate.
5. Place into buttered and floured ramekins, fill to the top and place on a baking tray.
6. Bake in a hot oven at 210°C for 7-10 minutes.
7. On removal from the oven dust with icing sugar and serve immediately.

NOTE:

Whilst I think the Toffoc is ideal in this recipe the alcohol can be changed to suite your palate, Grand Marnier or Cointreau being more traditional.

ROULADE GRIOTTINE

SERVES 8-10

ingredients

CHOCOLATE SPONGE:

130g Egg whites
63g Caster sugar
130g Egg yolks
40g Plain flour
17g Cocoa powder

DARK CHOCOLATE MOUSSE:

150g Callebaut 811 NV, 54% dark
   chocolate
300g Whipping cream
1 small jar Griottine cherries

method

CHOCOLATE SPONGE:

1. Whisk the egg whites and sugar to form a stiff meringue.
2. Add the egg yolks, then fold in the sieved flour and cocoa powder.
3. Spread onto a lined oven tray approximately 20x30cm and bake at 190°C for 12 minutes.

DARK CHOCOLATE MOUSSE:

1. Melt the dark chocolate to 45°C and fold in the lightly whipped cream, stirring continuously.
2. Spread half the chocolate mousse over the sponge then sprinkle the Griottine cherries on the top of the mousse.
3. Roll into a roulade.
4. Cover with the remaining chocolate mousse and finish with decorations of your choice or a few Griottine cherries.

CUP DENMARK

SERVES 6

ingredients

CHOCOLATE SAUCE:

160g Water
80g Whipping cream
1 Vanilla pod
300g Callebaut 811 NV, 54% dark
    chocolate
20g Butter

ASSEMBLY:

Vanilla ice cream
Whipped cream
Roasted flaked almonds

method

CHOCOLATE SAUCE:

1. Boil the water, cream and vanilla pod together.
2. Pour over the dark chocolate in a bowl.
3. Add the butter.
4. Mix well and serve hot.

ASSEMBLY:

1. Place the ice cream in a pre-chilled cup or glass.
2. Press a hollow in the ice cream with a spoon.
3. Decorate the edge with cream and sprinkle with the almonds.
4. Serve with a jug of hot chocolate sauce – to be poured in the hollow of the ice cream at the time of serving.

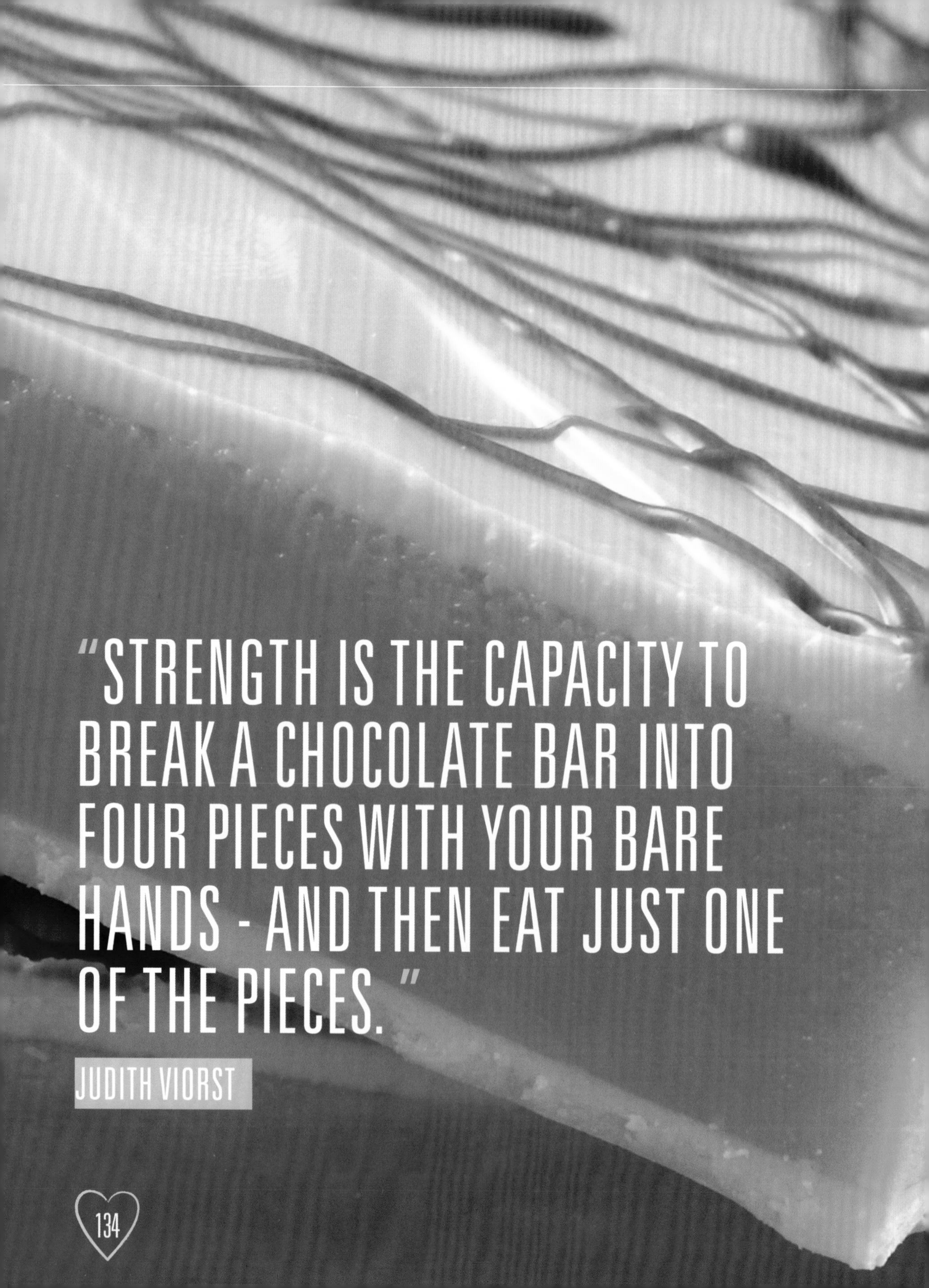

"STRENGTH IS THE CAPACITY TO BREAK A CHOCOLATE BAR INTO FOUR PIECES WITH YOUR BARE HANDS - AND THEN EAT JUST ONE OF THE PIECES."

JUDITH VIORST

134

BAKED LEMON AND
WHITE CHOCOLATE CHEESECAKE

FOR 8 GENEROUS PORTIONS

ingredients

BASE:

300g Ginger biscuits or speculaas
   biscuits
100g Chopped raisins, apricots
   and cherries
50g Flaked almonds
150g Butter, melted

CHEESECAKE FILLING:

300g Mascarpone cheese
200g Ricotta cheese
200ml Single cream
6 Free-range eggs, beaten
60ml Lemon juice
Grated rind of 2 unwaxed lemons
200g white chocolate, small pieces
   or callets

TOPPING:

Fruit glaze
Fresh raspberries, optional
Lemon zest, optional

TO SERVE:

Red fruit coulis
White chocolate decorations
Raspberries

method

BASE:

1. Grind the biscuits in a food processor and mix with the
    chopped fruit and flaked almonds. Add the melted butter and
    combine all the ingredients together. Place on the bottom of a
    24cm springform mould. Place in the fridge to harden.

CHEESECAKE FILLING:

1. Place all the cheese in a mixing bowl and at low speed with
    the spatula attachment pour in the cream then the beaten
    eggs, lemon juice and grated lemon rind. Fold in the
    bake-stable white chocolate chunks and pour the mixture
    on top of the refrigerated biscuit base.
2. Bake at 110°C for about 1 hour 15 minutes. Take out of the
    oven and allow to cool then refrigerate for at least 6 hours.

TOPPING:

1. Take out of the springform mould and brush the top with a
    fruit glaze. Decorate with fresh raspberries or just with some
    lemon zest.

TO SERVE:

1. Cut a wedge and serve with a red fruit coulis on the plate,
    a white chocolate decoration and some raspberries on top.

CARAMEL MOUSSE

ingredients

CARAMEL MOUSSE:

2 Leaves gelatine
100g Cream
200g Callebaut caramel flavoured
   chocolate
330g Semi-whipped cream

BISCUIT BASE:

250g Soft butter
150g Icing sugar
1 Small egg
400g Flour
70g Ground almonds
18g Corn flour
1 Pinch salt
125g Callebaut W2 NV
   white chocolate

method

CARAMEL MOUSSE:

1. Soak the gelatine leaves in cold water.
2. Bring the cream to the boil and add the gelatine to dissolve.
3. Pour the hot cream over the chocolate and mix until smooth.
4. Semi whip the 330g of cream and fold into the chocolate mix.
5. This makes 1 Demarle silicone mat with 8 indents (Charlotte mould).
6. Place in the freezer to set so you can turn it out.

BISCUIT BASE:

1. Mix the butter and icing sugar together, then add the egg and the rest of the ingredients.
2. Roll out and cut to shape, then bake at 180°C for about 15 minutes.

TO SERVE:

1. Sit the caramel mousse onto the sablé biscuit and garnish as you wish.

BITTER CHOCOLATE MOUSSE

SERVES 2

ingredients

100g 70% Amedei Venezuela
    Porcelana dark chocolate
Pinch of freshly ground nutmeg
2 Eggs, separated
2 heaped tsp Whipped cream
40g Grated dark chocolate and/or
    chopped toasted hazelnuts

equipment

2 stemmed wine glasses or ramekins

method

1. Melt the chocolate with the nutmeg before removing from heat.
2. Beat the egg yolks and add them to the chocolate while still hot, beating thoroughly.
3. Leave the mixture to cool for about 15 minutes.
4. Beat the egg whites to form soft peaks, then fold them into the chocolate mixture.
5. Spoon the mixture into the glasses, cover each with cling film and chill for about 2 hours until firm.
6. Top with whipped cream and some grated chocolate or chopped nuts.

DOUBLE CHOCOLATE BAKED CHEESECAKE

MAKES 6

ingredients

FILLING:

200g Full-fat cream cheese
50g Caster sugar
11g Cornflour
30g Fresh whole eggs
106g Whipping cream
80g Callebaut W2 NV white chocolate
40g Dark chocolate 70%

BASE:

70g Golden syrup
70g Unsalted butter
390g Digestive biscuit crumbs

method

FILLING:

1. Using a beater on slow speed, mix together the cream cheese, sugar and cornflour.
2. Add the eggs over 1 minute.
3. Now exchange the beater for the whisk and on second speed whisk until smooth.
4. Slowly add the cream while scraping down the bowl twice.
5. Put half the mix into another bowl.
6. Add the white chocolate to one half and the dark chocolate to the other.
7. Mix until clear.

BASE:

1. Melt together the golden syrup and butter and mix into the digestive crumb.
2. Place 26g of mix into a 7½cm diameter hoop placed on a silicone sheet on a baking tray. Press the crumb mix down firmly.
3. Place the cheesecake into two piping bags and deposit equal amounts of each flavour side by side into the hoops.
4. With a circular motion using a skewer, create a marble effect on the top.
5. Bake at 160°C for 35-40 minutes.
6. Probe the centre of the cheesecakes – they should reach 72°C.
7. Once baked this cheesecake can be frozen if required.

ORANGE AND GINGER
CHOCOLATE STEAMED SPONGE SERVED WITH DRAMBUIE CHOCOLATE SAUCE

MAKES 8 SMALL PUDDINGS

ingredients

ORANGE AND GINGER CHOCOLATE STEAMED SPONGE:

120g Butter
120g Caster sugar
100g Plain flour
1 tsp Baking powder
20g Cacao Barry Extra Brute
   Cocoa Powder
2 Large eggs
2 tbsp Full-fat milk
50g Crystallised ginger
Zest of 1 orange

DRAMBUIE CHOCOLATE SAUCE:

150g Callebaut 811 NV, 54% dark
   chocolate
150g Double cream
Drambuie, to taste

method

ORANGE AND GINGER CHOCOLATE STEAMED SPONGE:

1. Grease with butter 8 x dariole moulds.
2. Cream the butter and sugar together.
3. Gently add the sieved flour, baking powder and cocoa powder alternately with the beaten eggs and milk.
4. Gently stir in the ginger and orange zest.
5. Pipe the batter into the dariole moulds filling no more than three-quarters full.
6. Cover each mould with buttered greaseproof paper and tin foil, pressing the foil down the sides of each mould.
7. Steam for 40 minutes.
8. Unmould the hot puddings and serve immediately with Drambuie flavoured chocolate sauce.

DRAMBUIE CHOCOLATE SAUCE:

1. Put the chocolate and cream into a bowl.
2. Cook for 1 minute in a microwave at full power.
3. Stir well to create a smooth sauce.
4. Flavour with Drambuie to taste.

BELGIAN WAFFLES

BELGIAN WAFFLES

MAKES ABOUT 20 LARGE WAFFLES

ingredients

BATTER:

250g Plain white flour
25g Icing sugar
2g Salt
12g Fresh yeast
250ml Lukewarm water
250g Full-fat milk
2 Large free-range eggs
100g Butter, melted

WAFFLES:

Vegetable oil

TO SERVE:

Icing sugar
Ice cream, fruit, fruit coulis,
    chocolate or butter scotch sauce,
    as desired

method

BATTER:

1. Mix the flour, icing sugar and salt together. Dissolve the fresh yeast in the lukewarm water and add the milk. Pour the water/yeast milk mixture onto the flour/icing sugar/salt and whisk until smooth.
2. Beat the eggs until frothy and whisk into the batter. Finally whisk the melted butter into the batter. Place the batter in a warm place to allow it to double in volume.

WAFFLES:

1. Use an electric waffle maker. The waffle plates have to be very hot. Oil the plates with some vegetable oil.
2. Pour a ladle of batter onto each plate and close the waffle maker. Cook for 3-5 minutes until golden brown.

TO SERVE:

1. Dust with icing sugar, serve with ice cream, fruit, fruit coulis and/or a chocolate or butterscotch sauce.

CHOCOLATE SORBET

MAKES 1 LITRE 100ML

ingredients

700ml Water
260ml Granulated sugar
3 tbsp Glucose
100g Callebaut Madagascar
   dark chocolate
65g Cocoa powder

method

1. Boil the water, sugar and glucose for 5 minutes.
2. Remove from the heat and pour over the chocolate and stir until melted.
3. Sieve the cocoa powder into the chocolate mix and also mix until all combined.
4. Cool at room temperature then in a refrigerator until cold.
5. Freeze the sorbet in a ice cream machine following the manufacturer's instructions or in a container stirring every 30 minutes until smooth and creamy.

CHOCOLATE AND **PEAR**
BREAD **AND** BUTTER PUDDING

SERVES 6

ingredients

200g Callebaut 70-30-38, 70%
   dark chocolate
75g Butter
220g Caster sugar
425g Whipping cream
3 Whole eggs
1 Pinch Cinnamon
200g 3-day-old bread, sliced and
   crusts removed (250g loaf with the
   crusts removed)
2 Pears, peeled, poached and sliced
   into wedges (tinned pears can be
   used)

NOTE:

I prefer this pudding served hot
accompanied with a poached
pear and a pool of fresh cream (as
illustrated). However, if you assemble
and bake it in a shallow dish and
allow it to cool completely the
pudding can be cut into small cubes
or triangles and served as a canapé
dessert or as part of a trio of mini
chocolate desserts served together.

method

1. Melt together the chocolate, butter, sugar and cream in a plastic bowl in the microwave.
2. Whisk the eggs together with the cinnamon and add to the above mix.
3. Cut the bread into small squares or triangles and dip each piece into the mix, allowing a few seconds to absorb the custard.
4. Arrange into oven-proof containers interspersing with the drained sliced pears (either individual ramekins or larger dishes for multiple portions).
5. Pour over any remaining custard.
6. Bake at 180°C for 30-40 minutes (it is ready when it springs back when you press the middle, like a sponge cake).
7. Serve hot or cold.

NOTE:

"While I prefer to use plain white bread in this recipe because it is less sweet you can use brioche or panettone to create a softer, sweeter eat."

152

JAVA ORIGIN
MILK CHOCOLATE AND RUM GATEAU

SERVES 4

ingredients

DARK CHOCOLATE SPONGE:

4 Free range eggs
100g Caster sugar
Pinch salt
75g Self raising flour
50g Van Houten cocoa powder
Butter to grease the mould

GATEAU:

Dark rum, as required
250g Callebaut Origins Java milk
   chocolate mousse (see p126)
White and dark chocolate vermicelli
Some red berries, star fruit and
   chocolate curls to decorate
4 Square pieces dark
   chocolate sponge 3mm thick

method

DARK CHOCOLATE SPONGE:

1. Whisk the whole eggs with the sugar and salt until they have tripled in volume.
2. Sieve the flour and cocoa powder in a bowl.
3. Fold the flour and cocoa powder mix into the fluffy egg mixture.
4. Pour into a butter greased baking tin and bake for about 20 minutes at 200ºC.
5. Allow to cool for 20 minutes.
6. Turn over the baking tin onto a clean wire rack and allow to cool further before cutting.
7. Left over chocolate sponge can easily be frozen and used at a later date.

GATEAU:

1. Use a square tin about 10x10x10cm. Place the tin on a piece of plastic foil and place on the bottom a square of chocolate sponge soaked in dark rum. Pipe some mousse on the sponge and repeat four times. Finish the top of the tin by smoothing the mousse and place in the freezer.
2. After 4 hours take out the tin and with a gas blow torch heat the sides of the tin to loosen the cake. Take the cake out of the tin and allow it to defrost in the fridge.
3. Coat alternate sides with the white and dark vermicelli. Decorate the top with chocolate curls, the star fruit and some berries. When serving the gateau use a warm knife to cut it into portions.

CHOCOLATE NEMESIS

SERVES 10

ingredients

5 Whole eggs
100g Caster sugar
180g Caster sugar
125g Water
335g Dark chocolate 70%, melted
225g Unsalted butter

TO SERVE:

Vanilla ice cream

method

1. Whisk the eggs and 100g sugar together for 10 minutes.
2. Boil the 180g sugar and water together to 118°C.
3. Pour the boiled sugar into the egg mix.
4. Whisk until smooth.
5. Fold in the chocolate and butter.
6. Mix until smooth.
7. Pour the mix into ramekins.
8. Bake at 150°C for 45-50 minutes.
9. Serve with vanilla ice cream.

NOTE:

In the famous recipe from the 'River Café' this dessert is baked in a water bath, following the above recipe gives a more open texture to the cake which I think is preferable when served warm. Serve with a shot of chocolate sauce for added luxury.

MANGO MOUSSE
WITH A COCONUT FRIAND

8 INDIVIDUAL PORTIONS

ingredients

MANGO MOUSSE:

2 Leaves gelatine
240g Boiron mango purée
240g Cream

COCONUT FRIAND BASE:

200g Icing sugar
100g Coconut
60g Flour
150g Butter
150g Egg whites
Splash of vanilla

method

MANGO MOUSSE:

1. Soak the gelatine in cold water.
2. Melt the gelatine and add half of the mango purée.
3. Make sure the gelatine is all melted before adding the other half.
4. Fold in the semi whipped cream and pipe into a Demarle Flexipan (Ellipses shape).
5. Place in the freezer and allow to set before popping them out.

COCONUT FRIAND BASE:

1. Place the icing sugar, coconut and flour into a mixing bowl.
2. Melt the butter and add it to the flour mix.
3. Then add the whites and vanilla and pipe into a Demarle Flexipan (round cookie shape).
4. Bake in the oven at 180°C for 12-15 minutes or until golden brown.
5. Turn out and allow to cool.

TO SERVE:

1. Sit the mango mousse onto the friand and decorate as you wish.

CHARLOTTE VANILLA CHOCOLATE

SERVES 8-10

ingredients

CHOCOLATE SPONGE:

130g Egg whites
63g Caster sugar
130g Egg yolks
40g Plain flour
17g Cocoa powder

VANILLA MOUSSE:

60g Caster sugar
50g Egg yolks
250g Full-fat milk
½ Vanilla pod
5g (2½ Leaves) gelatine, soaked
   in water
250g Whipping cream

CHOCOLATE MOUSSE:

125g Callebaut Origins Java
   milk chocolate
125g Callebaut Origins Madagascar
   dark chocolate
500g Whipping cream

method

CHOCOLATE SPONGE:

1. Whisk the egg whites and sugar to form a stiff meringue.
2. Add the egg yolks, then fold in the sieved flour and cocoa powder.
3. Spread onto a lined oven tray and bake at 190°C for 12 minutes.
4. Cut a 4cm strip and line the side of a 20cm diameter by 4.5cm high cake ring. Cut two discs to fit inside the ring

VANILLA MOUSSE:

1. Whisk the sugar and the egg yolks together.
2. Boil the milk and the vanilla pod together, then add the egg yolks/sugar mix and cook until 75°C.
3. Add the drained gelatine leaves.
4. Leave to cool then mix in the whipping cream.
5. Place one sponge disc in the base of the ring and add the mousse. Place the second sponge disc on top of the vanilla mousse.

CHOCOLATE MOUSSE:

1. Melt the milk and dark chocolates to 45°C.
2. Fold in the lightly whipped cream.
3. Finish by piping the chocolate mousse over the top decoratively.

POACHED SPICED PEAR WITH VANILLA PARFAIT AND BITTER CHOCOLATE MOUSSE

POACHED SPICED PEAR WITH VANILLA PARFAIT AND BITTER CHOCOLATE MOUSSE

SERVES 4

ingredients

POACHED PEARS:

4 Small pears
250ml Red wine
1g Chilli flakes
1g Cinnamon
1g Star anise
Some cloves and black peppercorns
50g Caster sugar

PARFAIT:

4 Large free range egg yolks
75g Caster sugar
1 vanilla pod, seeds only
250ml Whipping cream

CHOCOLATE MOUSSE:

4 Free-range egg yolks
50g Caster sugar
100g Callebaut 70-30-38 NV
   dark chocolate, melted
4 Egg whites, whipped stiff

TO SERVE:

4 Squares 6x6cm milk chocolate
4 Squares 6x6cm dark chocolate
4 Chocolate sticks of about
   12cm long
Chocolate, melted, as required
Chopped hazelnuts, as required

method

POACHED PEARS:

1. Make these two days in advance so that the red wine can penetrate the core of the pear. Peel the pears, leaving the stem intact. Infuse the red wine with the spices and caster sugar and boil. Add the pears and simmer until the pears are cooked. Allow to cool and refrigerate.

PARFAIT:

1. Whisk the egg yolks with the caster sugar over a bain-marie until cooked. Add the vanilla seeds. Continue whisking until the mix is cool. Whip the cream until a soft peak is reached and fold gently into the egg mix. Pour into a bowl and freeze.

CHOCOLATE MOUSSE:

1. Whisk the egg yolks with the caster sugar in a bain-marie until thick and creamy. Fold in the melted chocolate and finally fold in the whipped egg whites. Pour into small glasses and refrigerate.

TO SERVE:

1. Take the squares of milk and dark chocolate and carefully cut out a little hole in the top right-hand corner (using a hot knife). Take the chocolate sticks and dip the ends into the melted chocolate and then into the chopped hazelnuts.
2. On an oblong plate place a spicy pear in the middle. Scoop out some of the vanilla parfait and place it between a milk and a dark chocolate square, press slightly so that the parfait is sandwiched between the two chocolate squares.
3. Push the chocolate stick through the holes to connect the two chocolate squares but not through the parfait. Place a glass with the bitter chocolate mousse on the right.

NOTE:

1. This recipe can be served with a red wine jelly made from the strained pear liquid. Simply bring the liquid to the boil, soak 4 gelatine leaves in water, squeeze out any excess and stir into the pear liquid. Pour into a tray and allow to set in the fridge. Serve by cutting into small squares of ½ cm, scattering four or five around the pear.

RASPBERRY CARDINAL

SERVES 10

ingredients

SWEET PASTRY:

100g Caster sugar
250g Unsalted butter
2 Whole eggs
350g Plain flour
Melted chocolate or cocoa butter,
  for brushing
Fresh raspberries

GANACHE:

250g Whipping cream
25g Liquid glucose
200g Callebaut 70-30-38 NV
  dark chocolate, chopped
80g Unsalted butter

DECORATION:

Fresh raspberries
Chocolate ruffles

method

SWEET PASTRY:

1. Mix the sugar and butter (at room temperature) together.
2. Add the eggs.
3. Add the sieved flour and bring to a paste without overworking.
4. Place into a plastic bag or wrap in cling film.
5. Refrigerate for at least 30 minutes.
6. Roll out the pastry using a minimum of flour.
7. Line a flan tin or dish with the pastry 23cm.
8. Place into the refrigerator to rest before baking to prevent shrinkage.
9. Bake blind using baking beans at 180°C for 10-15 minutes.
10. Once the pastry base is cool, brush the inside with melted chocolate or cocoa butter to prevent it becoming soggy.
11. Cover the base with the raspberries.

GANACHE:

1. Bring the cream and glucose to the boil.
2. Pour onto the chopped chocolate.
3. Mix until smooth.
4. Allow to cool then mix in the butter.
5. Pour over the raspberries and allow to set.
6. Decorate with fresh raspberries and chocolate ruffles.

166

NOTE:
The chocolate ruffles are created by spreading melted chocolate onto a frozen marble slab using a 'wall paper' style scraper with a handle. The chocolate sets straight away, cut into strips with the corner of the scraper, slide the scraper to release from the slab and manipulate and fold into a ruffle. Speed is important here and I would suggest a little practice wouldn't go amiss.

167

PASTRY

CHOCOLATE **TART**

CHOCOLATE **TART**

MAKES 15

ingredients

PASTRY:

A good 'short eating'
sweet pastry to line or
block into foil cases
(see recipe for
Raspberry Cardinal
(see p166)

FILLING:

450ml Whipping cream
400ml Full-fat milk
250g Callebaut 70-30-38 NV
    dark chocolate
10 Egg yolks
135g Caster sugar

method

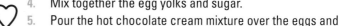

FILLING:

1. Bring the cream and milk to the boil.
2. Melt the chocolate.
3. Whisk the chocolate into the milk and cream mixture.
4. Mix together the egg yolks and sugar.
5. Pour the hot chocolate cream mixture over the eggs and sugar mix.
6. Return to the pan and bring back to the boil, whisking all the time.
7. This mix can be used straight away or may be cooled and refrigerated in a sealed container until required.
8. Lightly part bake the pastry cases.
9. Pipe the filling into the pastry cases (with a slight dome) – the yield is 30x10cm rounds or 4x25cm rounds.
10. Bake at 170°C for 25 minutes until set.
11. Allow to cool completely before adding chocolate decorations as desired.

NOTE:

Release your creative side by replacing the dark chocolate with white or caramel. Or we do a delicious 'chocolate orange tart' with the addition of a tangy orange curd in the base before the chocolate filling is piped in.

BRITTANY WITH
CHOCOLATE CREAM

8 INDIVIDUAL RINGS

ingredients

BISCUIT BASE:

130g Caster sugar
150g Butter
5g Salt
50g Egg yolks – base
200g Palin flour
3g Baking powder

CHOCOLATE CREAM:

125g Milk
125g Double cream
25g Sugar
50g Egg yolks
150g Callebaut 811 NV, 54% dark
   chocolate

method

BISCUIT BASE:

1. Mix together the sugar, butter and salt.
2. Add the egg yolks.
3. Then add the flour and baking powder.
4. Roll the mixture out to about a 2cm thickness.
5. Bake at 180°C for about 10-15 minutes or light brown.
6. When it comes out, cut with a round cutter or cut into squares.
7. Allow to cool and stand raspberries all the way around and fill with piped chocolate cream.
8. Garnish with crispy pearls.

CHOCOLATE CREAM:

1. Bring the milk and cream to the boil.
2. In a separate saucepan, mix together the sugar and yolks.
3. When the milk is boiling pour over the egg mixture.
4. Place it back onto the hob and cook out until it just about starts to boil.
5. Add the dark chocolate and allow to cool over night before piping.

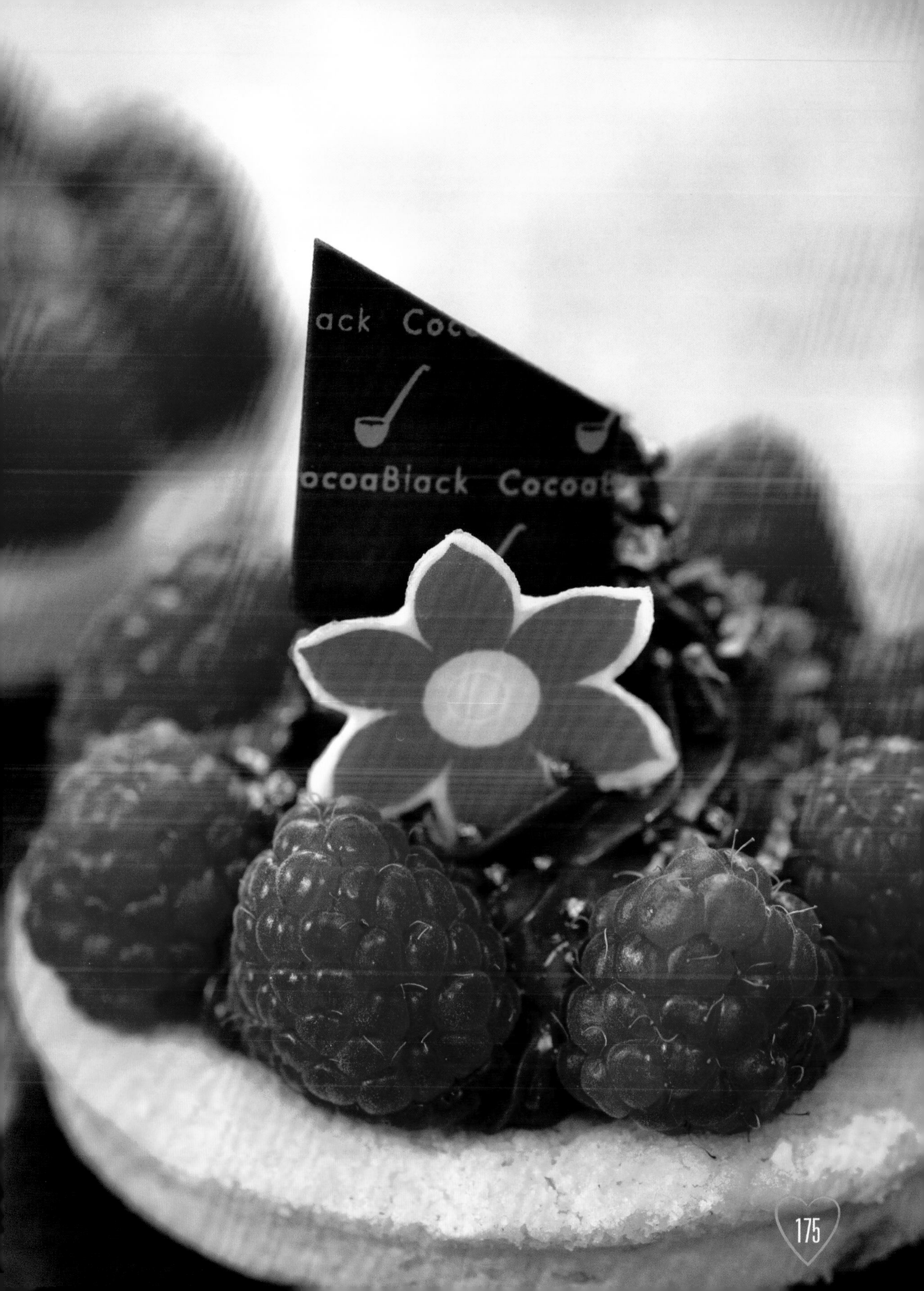

CHOCOLATE ECLAIR

CHOCOLATE ECLAIR

MAKES 20

ingredients

CHOUX PASTRY:

250g Water
100g Butter
4g Salt
2g Caster sugar
150g Plain flour
250g Whole eggs
Egg wash

CHOCOLATE PASTRY CREAM:

500g Full-fat milk
10g Butter
75g Whole eggs
100g Caster sugar
15g Cornflour
30g Plain flour
75g Callebaut 811 dark chocolate

GLAZE:

250g Full-fat milk
200g Callebaut 811 NV, 54% dark
  chocolate
150g Stock syrup
200g Bakers chocolate (pate
  a glacer)

method

CHOUX PASTRY:

1. Boil the water with the butter, salt and sugar.
2. Add the sieved flour and mix well.
3. Cook until smooth.
4. Place the mixture in a bowl and gradually add the eggs, beating well until shiny and smooth.
5. Pipe long éclair shapes onto a lined baking tray using a plain nozzle.
6. Apply egg wash and, using a fork, mark the top gently. This will prevent the éclair from losing its shape.
7. Bake in an oven at 190°C for 10 minutes and then lower the temperature to 160°C for a further 10 minutes (or more if necessary).

CHOCOLATE PASTRY CREAM:

1. Bring the milk and butter to the boil.
2. In a separate bowl, whisk the eggs and sugar together and add the sieved cornflour and flour
3. Add a third of the milk and the butter mixture to eggs and the flour mixture, combine and take back to the pan and bring to the boil.
4. Remove from the heat, add the chopped chocolate and leave to cool on a tray covered with a cling film.

GLAZE:

1. Bring the milk to the boil and pour over the finely chopped chocolate.
2. Add the syrup and finally the melted bakers chocolate. Make sure it is mixed well.
3. Leave to cool until it is slightly thickened so it will coat the top of the éclair.

TO FINISH:

1. When the éclairs are cold, cut down one side lengthways and fill with the chocolate pastry cream.
2. Glaze the top and decorate with chocolate.

DARK CHOCOLATE TART
INFUSED WITH COFFEE

MAKES 10 BANQUETTE-MOULDED (BOAT-SHAPED) TARTS

ingredients

SWEET PASTRY:

175g Plain flour
25g Cacao Barry Extra Brute
   Cocoa Powder
100g Butter
50g Caster sugar
50g Whole eggs

**DARK CHOCOLATE AND
COFFEE FILLING:**

200g Whipping cream
2 tsp Granular instant coffee
200g Callebaut 811 NV, 54% dark
   chocolate

DECORATION:

100g Callebaut 811 NV, 54% dark
   chocolate for piped decoration
10g Popping candy

method

SWEET PASTRY:

1. Sieve the flour and cocoa powder together.
2. Rub in the butter.
3. Dissolve the sugar in the eggs.
4. Mix together then place in a refrigerator for 1 hour.
5. Roll into desired tartlet cases.
6. Bake blind at 180°C for 10-15 minutes.

DARK CHOCOLATE AND COFFEE FILLING:

1. Bring the cream to the boil.
2. Stir in the instant coffee until dissolved.
3. Pour over the chocolate and allow to stand for a few minutes.
4. Stir to a smooth cream.
5. Set aside for 10 minutes.
6. Pour into the baked pastry cases and refrigerate for 2 hours.
7. Decorate with a piped lattice of pre-crystallised 811 NV, 54% dark chocolate sprinkled with popping candy.

"ANYTHING IS GOOD IF IT'S MADE OF CHOCOLATE."

JO BRAND

CHOCOLATE PECAN PIE

MAKES 20 TARTS

ingredients

CHOCOLATE PASTRY:

175g Plain flour
25g Cocoa powder
125g Margarine or butter
50g Caster sugar
2 Egg yolks
30g Water

CHOCOLATE PECAN FILLING:

350g Caster sugar
300g Maple or golden syrup
100g Butter
85g Cocoa powder
6 Eggs
8g Vanilla
400g Pecan nuts, chopped
Pecan halves for decoration
   (3 halves for each)
Apricot glaze, to finish

method

CHOCOLATE PASTRY:

1. Sieve the flour and cocoa powder together.
2. Rub in the fat.
3. Dissolve the sugar in the egg yolks and water, add to the mix and make up into a paste.
4. Refrigerate for at least 10 minutes to rest.
5. Block into foil cases or hand-lined tins (we use a 10cm tin foil case with a fluted crimp).

CHOCOLATE PECAN FILLING:

1. Warm and dissolve together the sugar, syrup and butter.
2. Add the cocoa powder, eggs and vanilla.
3. Stir in the chopped pecans.
4. Deposit the filling (70g) into the prepared pastry cases (10cm).
5. Decorate the top with three nuts halves.
6. Bake at 190°C for 20 minutes
7. Glaze when cool with an apricot glaze to seal the tart.

NOTE:

The filling can be made in a larger quantity and stored in a sealed container in the refrigerator for up to 2 weeks. Fresh tarts can be baked each day from this recipe (stir well each day before use as the mix tends to separate with standing).

184

PRALINE CHOCOLATE TART

PRALINE CHOCOLATE TART

SERVES 6

ingredients

SABLE PASTRY:

120g Butter
200g Plain flour
80g Icing sugar
20g Ground almonds
50g Whole eggs
Salt, to taste
Vanilla, to taste

VANILLA SPONGE SHEET:

500g Whole eggs
250g Caster sugar
160g Plain flour
50g Cornflour

FRANGELICO SYRUP:

100g Caster sugar
75g Water
40g Frangelico

PRALINE MILK CHOCOLATE GANACHE:

200g Callebaut 823 NV, 33% milk
  chocolate
50/60g Callebaut 811 NV, 54% dark
  chocolate
110g Praline nut paste
225g Whipping cream

method

SABLE PASTRY:

1. Preheat the oven to 180°C.
2. Rub the butter into the flour until sandy.
3. Add all the other ingredients and blend to a paste.
4. Roll out and cut to the size of six 10cm diameter tins.
5. Bake the pastry baked blind for 15-20 minutes.

VANILLA SPONGE SHEET:

1. Whisk together eggs and sugar in a bowl over a bain-marie until the mix reaches 35°C to make a basic génoise.
2. Remove from the heat and whisk until cold or a ribbon consistency.
3. Fold in the sieved flour and cornflour.
4. Pour onto a baking sheet 40x60cm and spread out evenly.
5. Bake in the oven at 200°C for 6-8 minutes.

FRANGELICO SYRUP:

1. Boil all the ingredients together for 1 minute exactly.

PRALINE MILK CHOCOLATE GANACHE:

1. Melt the milk and dark chocolate, add the praline nut paste and mix well.
2. Add boiled cream that has been cooled to 70-80°C and mix together.

ASSEMBLY:

1. Place a disc of sponge sheet on the base of the tartlet and brush over with Frangelico syrup.
2. Pour the ganache into the prepared tartlets.
3. Decorate to your choice or leave plain.

188

MILLEFEUILLE CHOCOLATE

SERVES 8-10

ingredients

PUFF PASTRY:

500g Puff pastry

PASTRY CREAM CHOCOLATE:

500g Full-fat milk
10g Butter
75g Whole eggs
100g Caster sugar
15g Cornflour
30g Plain flour
75g Callebaut 811 NV, 54% dark
  chocolate
Icing sugar
Cocoa powder

method

PUFF PASTRY:

1. Roll out to a 30cm square.
2. Leave to rest and bake in a hot oven to start (200°C) for 20 minutes, then turn down to 160°C for approximately 40 minutes. The pastry should be dry and crisp.
3. Leave to cool and cut into three strips approximately 10cm wide.

PASTRY CREAM CHOCOLATE:

1. Bring the milk and butter to the boil.
2. Whisk the eggs and the sugar together and add the sieved cornflour and flour.
3. Add a third of the milk and butter mixture to the eggs and flour mixture, combine and take back to the pan and bring to the boil.
4. Add the chopped chocolate and leave to cool on a tray covered with a cling film.
5. Divide the pastry cream mix into two portions.
6. Starting with pastry, spread one portion of pastry cream over the top, add the next strip of pastry, the second portion of pastry cream then finally the last pastry strip. Place in the fridge for 1 hour before decorating with icing sugar and cocoa powder.

CHOCOLATE ECLAIR

CHOCOLATE ECLAIRS

CHOUX PASTRY

MAKES 24 X 10CM ÉCLAIRS

ingredients

140g Strong flour
10g Cacao Barry Extra Brute
   Cocoa Powder
100g Butter
250ml Water
200g Eggs

method

1. Preheat the oven to 215°C.
2. Sieve the flour and cocoa powder.
3. Heat the butter and water slowly to boiling point, making sure the butter has melted.
4. Remove from the heat.
5. Stir in the sieved flour and cocoa powder.
6. Return to the heat and stir the mixture until it leaves the sides of the pan.
7. Remove from the heat and allow to cool to body temperature.
8. Add the beaten eggs one at a time until the mix falls from the spoon on a count of 5.
9. The quantity of eggs depends on the strength of the flour. The stronger the flour, the more eggs that are required.
10. Pipe straightaway onto a buttered floured tray/silpat mat/ demarle flexipan mat.
11. To make éclairs pipe out to 10cm long with a 1¼ cm plain nozzle.
12. Cook at 215°C for 15 minutes until brown and set.

CHOCOLATE PASTRY CREAM — CREME PATISSERIE

ingredients

40g Egg yolks (3 egg yolks)
50g Caster sugar
10g Plain flour
10g Cornflour
250g Full-fat milk
10g Butter
75g Callebaut 811 NV, 54% dark
   chocolate

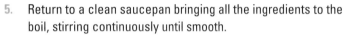

method

1. Whisk the egg yolks and sugar together.
2. Add the flours and mix to a smooth paste.
3. Bring the milk to the boil.
4. Allow the milk to cool slightly and then gradually add to the egg and sugar mixture, stirring well to create a smooth cream.
5. Return to a clean saucepan bringing all the ingredients to the boil, stirring continuously until smooth.
6. Pour into a bowl.
7. Gently stir in the butter and chocolate until melted.
8. Cover immediately with cling film to prevent a skin forming and condensation developing.

CHOCOLATE GLAZE FOR ECLAIRS

ingredients

150g Callebaut 811 NV, 54% dark
   chocolate
150g Double cream

method

1. Put the chocolate and cream into a bowl.
2. Cook for 1 minute in a microwave at full power.
3. Stir well to create a smooth glaze.

ASSEMBLY OF ECLAIRS:

1. Cut open the cooked éclairs along one side. Pipe in the chocolate pastry cream.
2. Dip the top of the éclair into the chocolate glaze. Enjoy!

"I WOULD GIVE UP CHOCOLATE BUT I'M NO QUITTER."

ANON

196

TEATIME
TREATS

HAZELNUT BROWNIES

MAKES ABOUT 20 BROWNIES

ingredients

150g Callebaut 811 NV, 54% dark
   chocolate
50g Praline paste
250g Butter
4 Whole free-range eggs
50g Ground hazelnuts
150g Plain flour
Chocolate bake-stable drops
Crushed hazelnut pieces
Icing sugar, to finish

method

1. Melt the chocolate with the praline paste in a microwave oven. Mix the butter with the eggs, then add the ground hazelnuts and flour. Add the chocolate and praline paste mix and stir until smooth.

2. Using a piping bag pipe the mixture into silicone moulds of your choice. Sprinkle some small chocolate bake-stable drops and crushed hazelnut pieces on top and bake for 15 minutes at 180°C. Allow to cool.

TO FINISH:

1. Just dust the brownies with some icing sugar.

GARDEN MINT TRUFFLE
HOT CHOCOLATE

SERVES 2

ingredients

1 full sprig (about 20g) of fresh
   garden mint (this can be
   substituted with 1 crushed stick of
   cinnamon)
100g Fresh full-fat milk
10g Fresh double cream
10g Honey
100g 72% Venezuela Araguani
   dark chocolate, melted
10g 33% Madagascar Tanariva
   milk chocolate, melted

method

1. Infuse the garden mint (or cinnamon) in the milk overnight.
2. Add the cream and honey and bring to just below boiling (approx 85°C).
3. Remove from heat and add the melted crystallised chocolates.
4. Mix with a hand blender.
5. Serve with additional fresh cream, sliced strawberries or a leaf of mint to garnish as desired.

MILLIONAIRE'S
SHORTBREAD

30 X 22CM FRAME (DEPENDANT ON SIZE OF PORTIONS)

ingredients

BASE:

450g Self raising flour
150g Caster sugar
300g Melted butter

CARAMEL:

100g Butter
75g Caster sugar
40g Golden syrup
200g Condensed milk

TOPPING:

Callebaut 823 NV, 33% milk
  chocolate, melted

method

BASE:

1. This makes a frame 30x22cm.
2. Place your flour and caster sugar into a mixing bowl.
3. Melt your butter and add it to the flour.
4. Mix well and pat into your baking tray or frame.
5. Bake at 160°C for about 15-20 minutes, it should be light brown.

204

CARAMEL:

1. Mix all the ingredients together and cook in the microwave.
2. It will take about 8-10 minutes but put it on in 1 minute intervals.
3. When it is a golden colour spread it onto the baked base and allow to cool.
4. Spread thinly with melted chocolate.

CHEWY CHOCOLATE OVERLOAD COOKIES

MAKES APPROX 30 BISCUITS

ingredients

125g Butter
250g Dark brown sugar
1 tsp Vanilla extract
1 Egg
150g Plain flour
35g Self-raising flour
1 tsp Bicarbonate of soda
35g Cacao Barry Extra Brute
   Cocoa Powder
100g Raisins
60g Dark chocolate chunks or buttons
60g Milk chocolate chunks or buttons
60g White chocolate chunks or
   buttons
100g Callebaut 811 NV, 54% dark
   chocolate callets

method

1. Preheat the oven to 180°C.
2. Beat the butter, sugar, vanilla extract and egg until smooth with an electric mixer.
3. Sieve together the flours, bicarbonate of soda and cocoa powder.
4. Stir into the creamed batter mixture.
5. Gently stir in the raisins, dark, milk and white chocolate chunks and dark chocolate callets.
6. Form into small rounds about the size of a walnut and place onto greased baking trays or silpat mats about 4cm apart. Flatten slightly.
7. Bake in the oven for 10 minutes. Cool for 5 minutes and then transfer to a cooling wire.
8. For the full impact of chewy chocolate sensation eat and enjoy while still warm!

MACAROONS

MAKES 50 TO 60 MACAROONS

ingredients

MACAROONS:

250g Ground almonds
450g Icing sugar
200g Egg whites
2g Cream of tartar
50g Caster sugar
Flavouring or food colouring

CHOCOLATE BUTTER CREAM:

100g Butter
20g Icing sugar
Flavouring, as desired
150g Callebaut W2NV white or
    811 NV, 54% dark, melted chocolate

method

MACAROONS:

1. Grind the ground almonds and the icing sugar finely in a food processor. Whisk the egg whites, the cream of tartar and half of the caster sugar. Using the rest of the caster sugar to further stiffen the egg whites as necessary. Add the flavouring or food colouring. With a spatula fold the almond/sugar powder until you have a smooth and shiny mixture.

2. Pipe macaroons on a silicone mat (2-3cm in diameter) and allow to crust for 30 minutes. Bake at 160°C for about 10 minutes. Allow to cool and store in air-tight containers until needed.

CHOCOLATE BUTTER CREAM:

1. Cream the butter with the icing sugar. Add any flavouring and with a spatula fold in the melted chocolate. With a piping bag fitted with a star nozzle pipe a rose onto a macaroon, place another macaroon on top and lightly press down.

NOTE:

This is an easy recipe for a chocolate butter cream that can also be used as a filling for a gateau or Swiss roll.

CHOCOLATE SPREAD

MAKES 475ML

ingredients

200ml Whipping cream
100g Callebaut 823 NV, 33% milk
    chocolate
75g Callebaut 811 NV, 54% dark
    chocolate
100g Unsalted butter

method

1. Boil the cream and remove from the heat and cool slightly, then pour over the milk and dark chocolates, stir until melted.
2. Cut the butter up into small cubes. place into the chocolate mix and mix until melted.
3. Place into a container in the refrigerator and leave to set overnight.

FLORENTINES

12 INDIVIDUALS

ingredients

250ml Cream
250g Granulated sugar
75g Butter
40g Liquid glucose
95g Honey
250g Flaked almonds
100g Raisins
Callebaut 811 NV, 54% dark
   chocolate, melted

method

1. Bring the cream, sugar, butter, glucose and honey up to the boil.
2. Boil until it just starts to turn a caramel colour.
3. Add the flaked almonds and raisins and scoop into silicone moulds.

4. Bake at 180°C until golden brown. This will take about 8-10 minutes.
5. Allow to cook and put melted chocolate at the bottom if you wish.

CHOCOLATE PECAN BROWNIES

MAKES 35

ingredients

200g Callebaut 70-30-38
   dark chocolate
125g Unsalted butter
225g Caster sugar
5g Vanilla paste
2 Whole eggs
1 Egg yolk
25ml Instant coffee, freshly made
135g Plain flour
5g Baking powder
1 Pinch salt
20g Cocoa powder
100g Pecan nuts, broken quite small

method

1. Line a 30x20cm roasting pan with foil.
2. On low power melt the chocolate in a plastic bowl in the microwave.
3. Cream the butter and sugar until light, then stir in the vanilla paste.
4. Add all the eggs in three portions, beating well between each addition.
5. Stir in the chocolate and the coffee.
6. Sieve the flour, baking powder, salt and cocoa powder together, then fold into the batter along with the pecans and mix through.
7. Deposit the mix onto a prepared baking tray and, using a palette knife, spread out evenly.
8. Bake at 180°C for 20-25 minutes.
9. When cold cut into small squares to serve.

NOTE:

If you wish to make a nut-free version substitute the nuts with chocolate chips to create a 'double chocolate' brownie. Or by using a combination of white, milk and dark chocolate you can create a delicious variation on a favourite.

SHORTBREAD
CHOCOLATE BISCUITS

MAKES BETWEEN 60 TO 80 BISCUITS

ingredients

550g Butter
225g Icing sugar
675g Plain white flour
1 Pinch salt
Vanilla extract
3 Egg whites

TO FINISH:

Cold dark chocolate sauce, to use as
   the filling
Melted chocolate
Chopped nuts such as hazelnuts,
   pistachios or almonds

method

1. Cream the butter with the icing sugar then add the flour, salt and vanilla extract and mix in. Then add the egg whites and mix further.
2. Use a star nozzle and pipe a variety of shapes onto silpats.
3. Decorate some with a half glacé cherry, bake-stable chocolate drops or leave plain.
4. Bake at 180°C for 8-10 minutes, remove from the oven and allow to cool.

DARK CHOCOLATE SAUCE OR DARK CHOCOLATE SPREAD

ingredients

200g Double cream
250g Callebaut dark chocolate
25g Butter

method

1. Pour the cream into a saucepan and bring to the boil. Whisk in the dark chocolate, 50g at a time until smooth and then add the butter. Store in the fridge until needed.

CHOCOLATE SAUCE:

1. Heat the mixture to 50°C and serve in a little jug.

CHOCOLATE SPREAD:

1. Pour the mixture into to a suitable container or glass jar and let it set in the fridge for a couple of hours before use.

SUGGESTIONS:

1. Add some grated orange zest and some orange liqueur to your mixture and pour over a good vanilla ice cream.
2. Add some crushed chillies for a spicy chocolate sauce or spread.
3. Whisk in some dark rum into the mixture allow to set in the fridge for a couple of hours, then with a melon ball, scoop some of the spread and roll the little balls through dark cocoa powder.

TO FINISH:

1. For the filling use the recipe for the dark chocolate sauce (see opposite). With a piping bag fitted with a star nozzle, pipe on a layer of the chocolate filling, place another biscuit on top and allow to set.
2. When set dip the ends of the biscuits in melted chocolate and sprinkle some chopped nuts on top. Store the biscuits in an air-tight container.

"CHOCOLATE DOESN'T MAKE THE WORLD GO AROUND ... BUT IT CERTAINLY MAKES THE RIDE WORTHWHILE!"

ANON

LENZ BURGERLI

MAKES 60

ingredients

60-75g Flaked almonds
Icing sugar, as required
100g Praline nut paste
200g Milk couverture (tempered)
50g Orange peel, finely chopped
Callebaut 823 NV, 33% milk
   chocolate, melted, for spreading
250g Gianduja (approximately)

method

1. Spread the almonds on to a silpat dusted well with icing sugar and roast at around 180-200ºC, mixing through from time to time.
2. Leave to cool.
3. Heat the praline nut paste to 30ºC, add the tempered chocolate and mix well to a smooth mass.
4. Fold in the cooled almonds and orange peel.
5. Place an 8 or 10mm high frame onto a plastic sheet, pour the mix on it and spread out level.
6. When set, thinly spread milk chocolate over the base, turn over onto a plastic sheet then cover the top with a thin layer of chocolate and mark to show the top or cover with a layer of gianduja.
7. Cut into petit four size squares or into 25x88mm bars.

ROCKY ROAD

30 X 22CM FRAME (DEPENDANT ON SIZE OF PORTIONS)

ingredients

BASE:

230g Milk chocolate
100g Butter
350g Digestive biscuits

TOPPING:

100g Butter
250g Callebaut 823 NV, 33% milk
   chocolate
200g Mini marshmallows
½ cup Walnuts, chopped
½ cup Cherries

method

BASE:

1. Melt the chocolate and butter together.
2. Crush up the digestive biscuits and mix in the chocolate and butter mix.
3. This makes a frame 30x22cm
4. Press the base into the frame and allow to set in the fridge.

TOPPING:

1. Melt the butter and chocolate.
2. Mix in the marshmallows, chopped nuts and cherries.
3. Press onto the base and allow to set for about 2 hours before cutting.

CHOCOLATE CAKE POPS

MAKES 25-30 CAKE POPS

ingredients

125g Unsalted butter
125g Caster sugar
2 Large eggs
100g Self-raising flour
25g Cocoa powder
125g Unsalted butter
200g Icing sugar
50g Cocoa powder
Chocolate, ideally tempered,
    for decoration
Sprinkles, optional

method

1. Preheat the oven to 170°C.
2. Cream 125g butter and the caster sugar together until light and fluffy.
3. Add the eggs one at a time until all combined.
4. Sieve the flour and 25g cocoa powder together and then fold into the egg mix.
5. Bake in a lined round baking tin about 18cm in diameter and cook for 25 minutes or until cooked.
6. Leave to cool and place in a food blender and make into cake crumbs (it is best to make the cake the day before).
7. To make the buttercream place the other 125g butter, icing sugar and 50g cocoa powder into a mixer and beat until light and creamy.
8. Add the cake crumbs and, using a large spoon, fold together – it should all come together like a thick paste.
9. Roll into small ball shapes about 5cm across.
10. Push the lolly sticks in each one with a little chocolate on the end and place on a tray and then in the fridge to rest harden for 1 hour.
11. Melt some chocolate in a bowl (for best results use tempered chocolate).
12. Dip each pop into the chocolate – they should set almost instantly.
13. To decorate pipe on small flowers or before the chocolate sets sprinkle with different sugar sprinkles.

SPICY HOT CHOCOLATE

SERVES ABOUT 8 TO 12

ingredients

SPICE MIX:

5g Chilli flakes
10g Cinnamon
5g Cloves
5g Black peppercorns
5g Nutmeg
5g Star anise

FOR 1 DRINK:

250ml Full-fat milk
50g Callebaut 70-30-38
   dark chocolate
2-4g Spice mix from ingredients
   above, to taste
Whipped cream or fluffy
   marshmallows, to serve

method

FOR 1 DRINK:

1. Steam the milk in a stainless steel jug. Add the dark chocolate and stir until dissolved.
2. Shake the spice mix into a tall latte glass. Pour the hot chocolate onto the spice mix and stir.

3. Decorate with whipped cream or marshmallows and serve.

CHOCOLATE FLORENTINES

MAKES 20

ingredients

150g 66% Mexique dark chocolate
150g 35% Papouasie milk chocolate
25g Chopped dried fruit
25g Whole nuts

method

1. Melt each chocolate separately in a microwave. Retain the temper by stirring frequently until it begins to melt. Stop heating when about 5-10% of the chocolate is still solid, which should then be dissolved by stirring it into the rest of the chocolate.

2. Pipe 10g, 3cm discs of chocolate onto silicone paper. Tapping the table will cause the discs to widen if desired.

3. Decorate with the dried fruit or nuts and gently press them into the surface. Aromatised crystallised flowers can also be used sparingly on thinner discs.

4. Place in a fridge for no more than 10 minutes and leave at room temperature for at least 3 hours.

CHOCOLATE MACAROONS
WITH GOLD LEAF

MAKES 15-20 MACAROONS

ingredients

PASTRY CREAM:

60g Caster sugar
2 Medium egg yolks
15g Cocoa powder
10g Custard powder
250ml Whipping cream
½ Vanilla pod and seeds

MACAROONS:

100g Egg whites
25g Caster sugar
120g Ground almonds
210g Icing sugar
20g Cocoa powder
Gold leaf, to decorate

method

PASTRY CREAM:

1. Whisk the sugar, egg yolks, cocoa powder and custard powder together in a bowl.
2. In a saucepan heat the cream with the vanilla pod and seeds until boiling. Remove and pour over the egg yolk paste.

3. Whisk in the bowl until everything is incorporated then return to the heat; keep stirring until the mix starts to get thick. Remove from the heat, pour into a bowl and allow to cool.

MACAROONS:

1. Preheat the oven to 130ºC.
2. In an electric mixer whisk the egg whites until light and fluffy, then add the caster sugar and keep whisking until glossy.
3. In a food processor blitz the almonds, icing sugar and cocoa powder together to a fine powder, fold in half the almond mix in, then the other half making sure not to over mix it, you should be looking for a smooth paste consistency.
4. Take a tray and place a sheet of silicone paper on top.
5. Pour the mix into a piping bag with an 8mm piping nozzle and pipe small round macaroons, keeping about 1cm between each one.
6. Place a small piece of gold leaf on top, then leave them to crust over before baking, this could take 10-40 minutes.
7. Bake in oven for 15-20 minutes.

ASSEMBLY:

1. When cooled pipe the pastry cream onto one of the macaroons and sandwich together with another.

DARK
HOT CHOCOLATE

MAKES 1 CUP

ingredients

300ml Hot milk
30g Callebaut 811 NV, 54% dark
  chocolate

method

1. Bring your milk up to the boil and pour into a coffee plunger.
2. Froth the milk by plunging the hot milk a few times.
3. Pour over the dark chocolate and whisk.

CHOCOLATE FRUIT SCONES

CHOCOLATE FRUIT SCONES

MAKES ABOUT 15 SCONES

ingredients

300g Plain white flour
100g Cold butter, cubed
100g Fruit mix (sultanas, glace
   cherries, mixed citrus peel)
50g Dark bake-stable chocolate
   chunks
1 Pinch salt
60g Caster sugar
8g Baking powder
190ml Buttermilk
1 Egg, beaten (egg wash) to brush
   the scones

TO SERVE:

Butter
Clotted cream
Raspberry jam

method

1. Rub 100g of white flour together with the cold butter cubes
   until you have a sandy texture. Add the rest of the flour, fruit,
   chocolate, salt, sugar and baking powder to the mix and mix
   in. Combine all these ingredients together with the buttermilk
   until you have a dough.

2. Flatten the dough to about 3cm thick and cut out scones.
   Place on a silicone baking sheet and brush with egg wash.
   Bake for about 25 minutes at 170°C.

TO SERVE:

1. Serve with butter, clotted cream and raspberry jam.

COLD HOT CHILLI CHOCOLATE DRINK

MAKES 8 SMALL GLASSES

ingredients

250ml Full-fat milk
½ Vanilla pod
1 Cinnamon stick 7½-10cm long
1 Small red chilli pepper, split with
  seeds removed
60g Callebaut 811 NV, 54% dark
  chocolate

method

1. Bring the milk to a simmer in a saucepan.
2. Add the split vanilla pod, whole cinnamon stick and red chilli pepper.
3. Add the chocolate and stir until melted.
4. Infuse all the ingredients for approximately 10 minutes.
5. Pass through a sieve to remove the spices.
6. Cool and refrigerate.
7. When you are ready to serve whisk to create a foam.
8. Serve poured over crushed ice.

"FORGET LOVE ...
I'D RATHER FALL IN CHOCOLATE!"

ANON

TABLES AND MEASURES

CONVERSION CHART WEIGHT (SOLIDS)

¼oz	7g
½oz	10g
¼oz	20g
1oz	25g
1 ½oz	40g
2oz	50g
2 ½oz	60g
¾oz	75g
3 ½oz	100g
4oz	110g
4 ½oz	125g
5 ½oz	150g
6oz	175g
7oz (2 cups)	200g
8oz (½lb)	225g
9oz	250g
10oz	275g
10 ½oz (3 cups)	300g
11oz	310g
11 ½oz	325g
12oz (¾lb)	350g
13oz	375g
14oz (4 cups)	400g
15oz	425g
1lb	450g
18oz	500g (1/2 kg)
1 ¼lb	600g
1 ½lb	700g
1lb 10oz	750g
2lb	900g
2 ¼lb	1kg

VOLUME (LIQUIDS)

1 teaspoon (tsp)	5ml
1 dessertspoon	10ml
1 tablespoon (tbsp)	15 ml or ½fl oz
1 fl oz	30ml
1 ½ fl oz	40ml
2 fl oz	50ml
2 ½ fl oz	60ml
3 fl oz	75ml
3 ½ fl oz	100ml
4 fl oz	125ml
5 fl oz	150ml or ¼ pint (pt)
5 ½ fl oz	160ml
6 fl oz	175ml
7 fl oz	200ml
8 fl oz	225ml
9 fl oz	250ml (¼ltr)
10 fl oz	300ml or ½ pint
11 fl oz	325ml
12 fl oz	350ml
13 fl oz	370ml
14 fl oz	400ml
15 fl oz	425ml or ¾ pint
16 fl oz	450ml
18 fl oz	500ml (½ ltr)
19 fl oz	550ml
20 fl oz	600ml or 1 pint

1 ¼ pints	700ml
1 ½ pints	850ml
1 ¾ pints	1 ltr
2 pints	1.2 ltrs
2 ½ pints	1.5 ltrs
3 pints	1.8 ltrs
3 1½ pints	2 ltrs
1 qt	950ml
2 qt	1 ltr
3 qt	2 ltrs
4 qt	3 ltrs
5 qt	4 ltrs

LENGTH

½ inch (")	5mm
½ inch	1cm
¾ inch	2cm
1 inch	2 1/2cm
1 ¼ inches	3cm
1 ¼ inches	4cm
2 inches	5cm
3 inches	7 ½cm
4 inches	10cm
6 inches	15cm
7 inches	18cm
8 inches	20cm
10 inches	24cm
11 inches	28cm
12 inches	30cm

OVEN TEMPERATURES

Celsius*	Fahrenheit	Gas	Description
110°C	225°F	Gas Mark 1/4	Cool
120°C	250°F	Gas Mark 1/2	Cool
130°C	275°F	Gas Mark 1	Very low
150°C	300°F	Gas Mark 2	Very low
160°C	325°F	Gas Mark 3	Low
180°C	350°F	Gas Mark 4	Moderate
190°C	375°F	Gas Mark 5	Moderate, Hot
200°C	400°F	Gas Mark 6	Hot
220°C	425°F	Gas Mark 7	Hot
230°C	450°F	Gas Mark 8	Very hot
240°C	475°F	Gas Mark 9	Very hot

* For fan assisted ovens, reduce temperatures by 10°C

TEMPERATURE CONVERSION C=5/9 (F-32)   F=9/5C+32

ACETATE
Sheets used for lining moulds and containers for a smooth finish.

AERATE
The process of allowing air to combine into ingredients to make then lighter and/or create more volume.

BAIN-MARIE
A container filled with hot water to cook or to hold at a temperature.

CALLETS
Chocolate callets are bits of chocolate, similar to chocolate chips in size, but without the traditional shape of a chocolate chip.

CARTOUCHE
A piece of baking paper, grease paper or wax folded three times and cut to the size required. Used to line a baking tin or cover a pan.

CONCERTINA
To fold, crush or push together.

COULIS
A thick sauce made of puréed fruit.

COUVERTURE
Chocolate that is a very high quality containing extra cocoa butter (32-39%).

DARIOLE MOULD
A cylindrical, slightly tapered mould for both cooking and serving individual desserts.

FEUILLETINE
A rough, crunchy textured biscuit.

FONDANT
1. A powdered form of icing sugar, but 100 times finer grind.
2. A smooth creamy mixture, often used as an accompaniment, filling or cake covering.

FRANGELICO
A hazelnut liqueur from Northern Italy.

FRIAND
A small French cake, often mistaken for a pastry.

GANACHE
A glaze, icing or filling made from chocolate and cream.

GENOISE
A very light Italian sponge cake closely associated with Italian and French cooking, forming the basic building block of much French pâtisserie.

GLAZE
A coating of glossy, often sweet, mixture applied to food.

GRIOTTINE CHERRIES
Cherries macerated in eau de vie or Kirsch.

INFUSE
To flavour or scent a liquid by steeping ingredients in it.

MERINGUE
A mixture of stiffly beaten egg whites and sugar, used as the basis for soufflés, sponges, pie and tart coverings or baked in small portions or large as a cake or a dessert.

MILLEFEUILLE
A pastry of French origin traditionally made up of 3 layers of puff pastry alternated with crème pâtissière.

MYCRYO®
Mycryo® is pure cocoa butter in dry, powder form, ideal for baking.

PALETTE KNIFE
A knife with a round-ended flexible blade used for scraping out a mixture from a bowl or spreading icing.

PARCHMENT PAPER
A cellulose based paper used in baking as a disposable non-stick surface.

PARFAIT
A frozen creamy dessert often served in slices or quenelles.

PRALINE
A confection made of nut kernels, especially almonds or pecans, stirred in boiling sugar syrup until crisp and brown.

PUREE
1. To blend or strain food until a thick consistency; 'blend until a purée'.
2. Food that has been blended or strained.

RAMEKIN
A small individual circular, porcelain glass or earthenware oven-proof dish.

ROSETTE
A rose-like shape.

ROULADE
A sponge cake or cake baked in a flat pan rolled around a filling.

ROYAL ICING
A hard, white icing made from softly beaten egg whites, icing sugar and sometimes lemon juice. Sets to a smooth, matte finish.

SABLE PASTRY
A sweet and sandy dough used for lining tarts.

SILPAT
A popular silicone mat used in baking to provide a non-stick surface without fat.

SNOBINETTE
A small hand dipped chocolate cup made to hold fondants, icings and creams.

SOUFFLE
A light, fluffy baked dish made with egg yolks and beaten egg whites.

SPRINGFORM MOULD
A type of bakeware that keeps the food in shape and features sides that can be removed from the base.

TEMPER
To bring chocolate to the desired consistency, texture or temperature.

TOFFOC
Toffee vodka from Wales.

VERMICELLI
Name given in the UK to small chocolate sprinkles.

WATER BATH
See bain-marie.

INDEX

INDEX

IF YOU LOVE 'I ♥ CHOCOLATE' WHY NOT TRY THESE...

CHOCOLATE COOKBOOKS

As one of the UKs favourite ingredients – chocolate recipes are popular with consumers of all ages. Whether bite-size pralines, dramatic cakes or as indulgent desserts – chocolate is an all-round winner. Now thanks to programmes such as 'BBC One's 'MasterChef' the art of the chocolatier is becoming more and more popular with the public.

Whether learning the basics such as how to temper, layering or fill the preparation and creation of chocolate designs and dishes are a must-have choice for celebratory events and dinner parties. Chef Book's collection of chocolate-focused books are suitable for chocolate novices and chocolate professionals – providing a great range to encourage this growing skill.

CHOCOLATE TO SAVOUR

AUTHOR: KIRSTEN TIBBALLS

- The cookbook from Australian celebrity chocolatier Kirsten Tibballs, guest judge on 'MasterChef Australia'
- All the recipes from Melbourne's Savour kitchen and chocolate school
- Offers budding and professional chocolatiers the opportunity to recreate mouth-watering dishes at home
- Includes pralines, macaroons and Kirsten's renowned celebration cakes.

RRP Price: £70.00

ISBN: 978-1-908202-13-0

CREATIVE CHOCOLATE BY JOHN SLATTERY

AUTHOR: JOHN SLATTERY

- Dishes created by master chocolatier John Slattery
- Featuring a selection of treats from his iconic chocolate shop Slattery's in Manchester
- Learn the basics of chocolate making with easy-to-follow rules
- Indulge your tastebuds with tempting chocolate recipes
- Recreate Slattery's stunning celebration cakes for weddings or other events

RRP Price: £25.00

ISBN: 978-1-908202-07-9

A WORLD OF CHOCOLATE

For many chocolatiers and pastry chefs around the globe the World Chocolate Masters is the highlight of the year, with contenders training over many months to showcase the very highest standard of chocolate development. Pitting themselves against fellow competitors all of the world, 19 countries battle it out to become World Chocolate Master.

Consisting of moulded and coated pralines, entrements and plated desserts *A World of Chocolate* offers an insight into the preparation and creativity of the world's best chocolatiers. Available in 9 languages, *A World of Chocolate* is a inspirational source of flavour, styles and techniques – making this a chocolatiers bible.

A WORLD OF CHOCOLATE STANDARD

AUTHOR: VARIOUS

- Over 65 winning recipes recipes from the entrants of The World Chocolate Masters
- Includes a collection of entrement, dessert and coated and moulded praline recipes
- Perfect for those in the chocolate industry looking for inspiration, designs and flavours
- Includes biography of each winner and history of the competition

RRP Price: £25.00

ISBN: 978-0-9567667-6-2

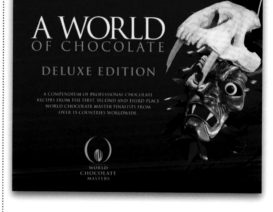

A WORLD OF CHOCOLATE DELUXE

AUTHOR: VARIOUS

- The must-have chocolate compendium for chocolate professionals
- Features over 150 World Chocolate Master recipes
- Includes recipes from the 18 qualifying winners but also recipes from the second and third place contestants.

RRP Price: £55.00

ISBN: 978-0-9567667-3-1